Controls, Procedures and Risk

AF677248

Butterworth-Heinemann – The Securities Institute

A publishing partnership

About The Securities Institute

Formed in 1992 with the support of the Bank of England, the London Stock Exchange, the Financial Services Authority, LIFFE and other leading financial organizations, the Securities Institute is the professional body for practitioners working in securities, investment management, corporate finance, derivatives and related businesses. Their purpose is to set and maintain professional standards through membership, qualifications, training and continuing learning and publications. The Institute promotes excellence in matters of integrity, ethics and competence.

About the series

Butterworth-Heinemann is pleased to be the official **Publishing Partner** of the Securities Institute with the development of professional level books for: Brokers/Traders; Actuaries; Consultants; Asset Managers; Regulators; Central Bankers; Treasury Officials; Compliance Officers; Legal Departments; Corporate Treasurers; Operations Managers; Portfolio Managers; Investment Bankers; Hedge Fund Managers; Investment Managers; Analysts and Internal Auditors, in the areas of: Portfolio Management; Advanced Investment Management; Investment Management Models; Financial Analysis; Risk Analysis and Management; Capital Markets; Bonds; Gilts; Swaps; Repos; Futures; Options; Foreign Exchange; Treasury Operations.

Series titles

■ **Professional Reference Series**
The Bond and Money Markets: *Strategy, Trading, Analysis*

■ **Global Capital Markets Series**
The REPO Handbook
Foreign Exchange and Money Markets: *Theory, Practice and Risk Management*
IPO and Equity Offerings
European Securities Markets Infrastructure
Best Execution in the Integrated Securities Market

■ **Operations Management Series**
Clearing, Settlement and Custody
Controls, Procedures and Risk
Relationship and Resource Management in Operations
Managing Technology in the Operations Function
Regulation and Compliance in Operations
Understanding the Markets

For more information

For more information on **The Securities Institute** please visit their web site:

www.securities-institute.org.uk

and for details of all **Butterworth-Heinemann Finance** titles please visit Butterworth-Heinemann:

www.bh.com/finance

Controls, Procedures and Risk

David Loader

BUTTERWORTH
HEINEMANN

OXFORD AMSTERDAM BOSTON LONDON NEW YORK PARIS
SAN DIEGO SAN FRANCISCO SINGAPORE SYDNEY TOKYO

Butterworth-Heinemann
An imprint of Elsevier Science
Linacre House, Jordan Hill, Oxford OX2 8DP
200 Wheeler Road, Burlington MA 01803

First published 2002

Copyright @ 2002, David Loader. All rights reserved

The right of David Loader to be identified as the author of this work has been asserted in accordance with the Copyright, Designs and Patents Act 1988

No part of this publication may be reproduced in any material form (including photocopying or storing in any medium by electronic means and whether or not transiently or incidentally to some other use of this publication) without the written permission of the copyright holder except in accordance with the provisions of the Copyright, Designs and Patents Act 1988 or under the terms of a licence issued by the Copyright Licensing Agency Ltd, 90 Tottenham Court Road, London, England W1T 4LP. Applications for the copyright holder's written permission to reproduce any part of this publication should be addressed to the publisher

British Library Cataloguing in Publication Data
Loader, David
Controls, procedures and risk. – (Operations management series)
1. Financial services industry – Management 2. Risk management
I. Title II. Securities Institute
332.1'068

Library of Congress Cataloguing in Publication Data
A catalogue record for this book is available from the Library of Congress

ISBN 0 7506 5486 4

For information on all Butterworth-Heinemann finance publications visit our website at: www.bh.com/finance

Composition by Genesis Typesetting, Rochester, Kent

Transferred to Digital Printing in 2008

Contents

With thanks to Computer Based Learning Ltd and the dsc.portfolio,
and special thanks to Rachel Davis and Caroline Parish for assistance in compiling the content

Preface

In the financial services industry risk is a constant threat to organizations of all sizes and to the markets themselves. Many industry 'events' have shown how dangerous it is when a business operates in an uncontrolled way, particularly when the lack of control was not evident to the management of the business until it was too late.

Case studies of the most publicized problems mostly point to the exposures in products that are either too large for the potential losses to be sustained by the business or exposures that have been taken by traders, dealers or fund managers that are not recorded or hidden from management, the so-called rogue trader.

However, we should not assume that all risk is associated with dealing. In fact much of the risk that firms face is created by the failure of processes, systems and management, in other words, operational risk. When operational risk like the failure of a process to identify a trading position occurs it is not standalone. The risk is magnified by the fact that not only is there an unidentified trade but there is now also a risk that a loss will occur on that trade, in other words, a market risk. Being unaware of the position, the managers cannot mitigate against any adverse market movement and so the business is exposed to potentially unlimited losses.

It is clear from the papers published by the Bank for International Settlement and the Basle Committee, and indeed many other eminent organizations and industry bodies, that operational risk is considered a serious issue in the industry and that it ranks along with market and credit risk in importance. As Operations teams are therefore involved in the process of managing operational risk we need to consider how exactly the risk arises, what is needed to identify the risk and measure its impact and finally how the risk is to be controlled. Yet operational risk is something that has existed ever since the first trade was carried out and the components that are associated with Operations such as settlement risk, the risk of a failure or problem with settlement of a trade, is hardly something that is new to most Operations teams. We need to be careful that we understand exactly what we mean by the terms operational risk as well as other types of risk like market, credit, legal, etc.

For instance, consider the following:

> **Publicised losses in this five-year period (1993 to 1997) arising from misuse of, or other problems associated with, derivatives amounted to approximately $23.3 billion**
>
> ***(Source: Capital Market Risk Advisors/Euromoney)***

Taken by itself this sounds like a very, very significant figure. However, the key is what was the value of derivative business in that same period. If, as was the case, the value was enormous and this $23.3 billion represents a small percentage, the risk is put into a different context. We must also not forget that much of the business in financial markets is about trading risk, taking risk and managing risk. We do not seek to remove risk in every circumstance and situation and yet it is imperative that we know what the risk is and where we do want to manage that risk out of the situation, we are able to do so.

The risk profile of an organization is important particularly as that risk profile may be very different for each of the business areas within that organization. A clearing-house manages risk, a fund manager takes various risk views, a principal trader makes money from taking a risk on market movements while an arbitrageur takes a 'risk-free' strategy. Within an investment bank, then, there are different risk profiles and they are reflected in the products traded and the exposures taken.

We noted earlier that risk is not only about trading and operational risk is significant. So too is the risk associated with clients and other counterparties. This credit or counterparty risk is very much about the risk of default on obligations but it should also relate to the impact that the counterparty has on the operational risk of the firm dealing with them.

If a client is poor in terms of its administration capability then it will impact on the broker dealing for them. Late settlement, missed or incorrect instructions and payments etc. will, at the very least, add to cost and could possibly be more significant.

Risk is a massive subject covering so many sources and types and each with a different potential impact. Many of those risks are part of the business and therefore can be managed by having robust and workable procedures and controls. The Operations managers and supervisors have a role here and the Operations team the responsibility to ensure that the procedures and controls are implemented, maintained and managed.

Sadly there are also other risks that are less predictable and yet devastating: 11 September 2001 graphically showed the need for adequate disaster recovery and business – continuation policies. Fraud, money laundering and system hacking all represent risk to an organization.

Risk is clearly an issue but so too is control over that risk. The way in which each organization approaches the control of the risk it faces will be a mix of mandatory strategy dictated by regulation and industry best practice and bespoke control based on the company, its risks and its infrastructure. Obviously a small company cannot introduce controls like segregation as easily or effectively as a much larger organization. On the other hand, the risks faced by the smaller business should be more easily identified and managed.

The controls needed for, say, payments will be different from the controls over the systems so the overall policy on procedures and controls becomes a case-by-case scenario in the Operations function and one that needs constant monitoring for effectiveness and relevance as well as ensuring that the personnel are fully risk aware. This represents a major challenge to the managers to produce procedures and controls that will be suitable and yet are robust, that can be flexible and yet effective.

Compiling and documenting procedures will be time consuming and yet it is imperative that this happens if the controls are to work and that the risk management process can be demonstrated to interested parties such as the regulators, audit and even potential counterparties. Today the use of external companies to document the procedures is often utilized and the decision to seek an independent review of the procedures themselves is prudent.

Controls, procedures and risk are occupying more and more management time. The responsibility to manage the risks lies with the whole Operations team. If it is successful in fulfilling this role the overall risk of the business is reduced, if it is not successful the consequences may be severe.

In this book I have deliberately focused on the subjective or practical side of risk, controls and procedures. However, rather than analyse the Basel Capital Accord and the capital requirements etc., (updates and information on the Accord[1] are contained in Appendix 1), I want

[1] See the website address for the Bank for International Settlements (www.bis.org)

to focus operations personnel on the aspect of risk management that, in operations risk terms, is critical; the 'gut feel' of experienced people.

I do not wish in any way to suggest that the mathematical approach to operational risk is not important because clearly it is. Operational risk modelling is part of the risk management process and there are many articles, papers and publications that cover the subject. Indeed later in the book we look at Standards for the Control of Operational Risk and again Appendix 2 contains detail of this risk management tool. It is my view, and it is a view shared by many, that risk and controls and procedures in an Operations context are a very different animal from those in market and credit risk. Controls and procedures in the clearing and settlement functions are about efficiency as much as risk management, and yet they are, in most cases, quite effective in controlling risk. Efficient procedures and controls enhance profitability, the fact they manage risk as well is a bonus. In reality we have controls and procedures that are process based and controls and procedures that are risk based, and some that are both.

There is a problem with this. We can end up with too many procedures and controls and rather than reducing risk they actually create greater risk by sometimes confusing and contradicting other procedures and controls. There is also the need to recognize the characteristics of products and services and their associated risks. For example, derivatives are often perceived as high risk and yet in clearing and settlement terms many derivatives are far less of a risk because of central clearing counterparty processes and margin disciplines than settlement of equities and bonds.

There is no doubt that overkill in terms of attempting to control operational and operations risk is a real possibility. I have seen situations where there are so many controls and procedures in place that in order to process the business they are ignored or circumvented. What is the use of a policy that actually increases risk rather than achieving what it is supposed to do and manage risk?

Operations teams need to be aware of risk but not overwhelmed by it. Nowhere is risk in operations and operational terms going to be eradicated. However, in the successful organizations that are efficient and cost effective (profitable) the risk of financial loss or reputation loss is very successfully identified and managed so that while it is always there it manifests itself infrequently and is quickly dealt with.

At the end of the day the successful Operations manager will have created a highly efficient Operations team working with controls and procedures that are relevant, workable and effective. As a result that manager will also have controlled Operations risk and therefore contributed to the management of operational risk.

That success will have little to do with risk models and everything to do with skills, experience and management capability. The greatest risk management tool in any organization is its people.

Chapter 1

'Against the Gods'

The title of this chapter is taken from the worldwide bestseller *Against the Gods – The Remarkable Story of Risk* by Peter L Bernstein. This excellent book highlights many interesting facts about the approach to risk including an ingenious bond issued by the Confederates in the US Civil War that encompassed several attractions for potential investors. The risk was, of course, that the Confederate States would lose and the bonds would become worthless. To overcome that risk issue the bonds were convertible into cotton and the payments would be in either pounds sterling or French francs. Thus an early 'derivative' incorporated an insurance policy. The constant search for investment that is safe yet still provides an adequate return occupies the minds of investors and the providers of the instruments for the investment. Financial markets are essentially a remarkable story of risk in their own right, as several high-profile events have proved. The crazy speculative investments of years ago are mirrored to some degree by the crazy investment in hugely overpriced technology and communication companies in the last few years. The dot-com bubble made many staggeringly rich at the expense of the many more losers. Yet it would be wrong to consider that financial markets are solely about the investment risk. Any investment carries an element of risk that is not connected with the mechanics of the market, i.e. price, but is related to other types of risk such as loss of benefits that are due on a security or the loss of a bearer security.

Gold, historically, is often used as an investment in times of war or other global tension perhaps in the belief that if cash becomes impossible to use then gold would become the 'currency' of the world. Other aspects of commerce and daily living carry risk. A commodity farmer runs a risk because the crop may be poor, so too does a homeowner because the property could be damaged or burgled. A driver of a car is at risk, a motorcyclist at a greater risk. In many cases the natural way to mitigate that risk is to have insurance. Thus we have house insurance, car insurance, life insurance, credit card insurance, etc.

Lloyd's of London is synonymous with insurance. As the largest insurance market in the world this is hardly surprising and yet insurance is itself not without risk. The Lloyd's market is something most have heard about but few understand. The way Lloyd's works and the crisis that affected it are worth studying as it provides an insight into the theory of risk and risk aversion that underpins the whole controls and risk management process.

Exactly when Lloyd's was formed in London is not known. However, Thomas Lloyd's coffee shop is recorded as being in existence in the seventeenth century and that is when Lloyd's business is generally recognized as being founded. Lloyd's is not an insurance company but is a cooperative of writers of insurance known as 'names'. Individuals that join Lloyd's as a name form syndicates that write the insurance.

This is a very important process as the syndicate obviously shares the risk that one name would otherwise have. Syndicates could also lay off some of the risk to other syndicates, thus spreading the risk wider but reducing the impact of paying out on a claim.

Just about anything can be insured at Lloyd's although its early development revolved around insuring ships. The Lutine Bell that is still used was rung in the Lloyd's building when the loss of a ship was received. The names in the syndicate make their money, often quite considerable sums, if the claims on the insurance they write are low but should a catastrophe occur and they are the writers of the relevant insurance they can lose substantial amounts. Lloyd's names have unlimited liability and should a major catastrophe occur then they may lose their homes in paying out on the claim. This happened to a few unfortunate syndicates with claims against them for the effects of asbestos that ran into millions of pounds. Today it is possible for a company to become a corporate name of Lloyd's and they represent a very substantial percentage of the insurance capacity Lloyd's offers.

Lloyd's then offers both the infrastructure for insurance to be purchased (names) and also the means to reduce the risk of writing the insurance (syndicates).

As Lloyd's names are aware, risk events happen. They are caused by something and yet that something can be obscure. The UK stock market crash of 1987 resulted in a fall of over 20% in the month of October. Such a fall had occurred only a handful of times before and this collapse came from seemingly nowhere. There were theories but the true reasons for the crash were and remain obscure. When we look at different risks such as market or credit risks there are certain fundamental elements of the risk that can be identified and measured.

Understanding the risks in financial markets involves looking at case studies of when, how and why a risk manifested itself and what the impact was. One significant risk event involved the collapse of a long-established bank in the UK, Barings Bank.

Barings' collapse was due to the unauthorised and ultimately catastrophic activities of, it appears, one individual that went undetected as a consequence of a failure of management and other controls of the most

> **basic kind. Management failed at various levels and in a variety of ways, described in the earlier sections of this report, to institute a proper system of internal controls, to enforce accountability for all profits, risks and operations, and adequately follow up on a number of warning signals over a prolonged period. Neither the external auditors or the regulators discovered Leeson's unauthorised activities.**
>
> (Report of The Board of Banking Supervision Inquiry Into The Collapse of Barings, 18 July 1995)

This statement encapsulates the issue of risk in financial markets, showing as it does the near-total failure of every basic control that should be in a business such as a bank. The catastrophic activities were, of course, taking positions, very large positions, in markets that gave the bank an exposure to subsequent movement in the markets. The losses generated by these activities were as much caused by poor judgement and bad luck in the market as by the ability of a trader to hold positions and therefore exposure to the market for Barings without management being aware. The frightening possibility is that had the Japanese market where Leeson had built up this huge exposure moved the opposite way, the world might never have heard about Leeson and would still not be aware of the inherent danger that is posed not just by market and credit issues but also by operational risk issues.

As it was serious, question marks were raised about regulation and management in the financial markets and the whole question of risk and particularly operational risk was elevated in importance.

The following definition of operational risk by the Basel Committee of the Bank for International Settlement (BIS) is one of the outcomes of the deliberations about the collapse of Barings and other events in the industry. To illustrate why the definition was published I am including the background and rationale for the operational risk charge. The following details have been obtained from the excellent Bank For International Settlement website (see the Appendix for details) where there are papers and updates on many other interesting subjects

Background and the rationale for an operational risk charge

In recent years, supervisors and the banking industry have recognized the importance of operational risk in shaping the risk profiles of financial institutions. Developments such as the use of more highly automated technology, the growth of e-commerce, large-scale mergers and acquisitions that test the viability of newly integrated systems, the emergence of banks as very large-volume service providers, the increased prevalence of outsourcing and the greater use of financing techniques that reduce credit and market risk, but that create increased operational risk, all suggest that operational risk exposures may be substantial and growing.

This recognition has led to an increased emphasis on the importance of sound operational risk management at financial institutions and to greater prominence of operational risk in banks' internal capital assessment and allocation processes. In fact, the banking industry is currently undergoing a surge of innovation and development in these areas.

Reflecting these developments, the Basel Committee on Banking Supervision established the principle of developing a Pillar 1 minimum regulatory capital charge for other risk, including operational risk, in its 1999 Consultative Paper. Following the consultation process and its own analysis, the Committee decided that only operational risk should be subject to a capital charge under Pillar 1.

Additional elements of 'other risk' – for instance, interest rate risk in the banking book and liquidity risk – will be dealt with solely through Pillars 2 and 3. This position was expressed in the January 2001 Consultative Package and forms the assumption underpinning the Risk Management Group's (RMG's) ongoing analysis.

This paper contains an overview of the RMG's work to date on refining the proposals for a Pillar 1 regulatory minimum capital requirement for operational risk. It reflects the RMG's extensive contact with financial industry representatives, its review of the many thoughtful and constructive comments received on the January Consultative Package, and the RMG's own internal deliberations. This work has resulted in a number of significant changes to the January proposals. These changes include

- Refinement of the definition of operational risk that underpins the regulatory capital calculations
- Proposed reduction in the overall level of the operational risk capital charge
- Introduction of a new regulatory capital approach that is based on banks' internal risk estimates (the 'Advanced Measurement Approaches' (AMA) and
- Consideration of the role of insurance as a risk mitigant in the regulatory capital calculations.

These changes are described more fully in the sections that follow. The RMG intends to continue work to refine these proposals in the light of industry comments and with the benefit of tranche 2 Quantitative Impact Study (QIS) data that it will review further over the course of the autumn.

Definition of operational risk

In the January 2001 Consultative Package, operational risk was defined as: 'the risk of direct or indirect loss resulting from inadequate or failed internal processes, people and systems or from external events'. The January 2001 paper went on to clarify that this definition included legal risk, but that strategic and reputational risks were not included in this definition for the purpose of a minimum regulatory operational risk capital charge.

This focus on operational risk has been generally welcomed, although concerns were expressed about the exact meaning of 'direct and indirect loss'. As mentioned above, for the purposes of a Pillar 1 capital charge, strategic and reputational risks are not included, and neither is it the intention for the capital charge to cover all indirect losses or opportunity costs. As a result, reference to 'direct and indirect' in the overall definition has been dropped. By directly defining the types of loss events that should be recorded in internal loss data, the RMG can give much clearer guidance on which losses are relevant for regulatory capital purposes. This leads to a slightly revised definition, as follows: 'the risk of loss resulting from inadequate or failed internal processes, people and systems or from external events'. The RMG confirms that this definition does not include systemic risk and the operational risk charge will be calibrated accordingly.

What does this mean for operations teams? Essentially it means that there are situations that will be defined as risk and that will have a bearing on the capital charge requirements of the firm. The operations manager has now to analyse the procedures, processes and risks based on various considerations and in particular to identify 'operational risk' as defined above and 'operations risk', which is the risk of problems with procedures and processes as part of the everyday clearing, settlement and administration process carried out by the operations teams.

There has been a significant shift in the regulatory and best practice approaches in the industry. Organizations of all types have operations teams that handle a wide variety of functions and processes and also develop procedures to control the efficiency and any risk associated with the processes. Other areas of the business manage non-operational risks that a business could face so that for instance market risk issues are managed by management teams, compliance and to some extent audit. A credit department, for example, manages risk issues affecting the exposure to a particular counterparty such as a client.

In looking at the characteristics of risk in the financial markets it is reasonable to say that there are three main risk categories, which are market, credit and operational risk. Within each main category are numerous sub-categories of risks as Table 1.1 shows.

Table 1.1 Sub-categories of risk

Business	Counterparty
Market Associated	Regulatory
System	Reputation
Personnel	Fraud
Settlement	Disaster Recovery
Financial	Legal

This list of sub-categories is not exhaustive and these sub-categories themselves can be broken down further so that an organization has the ability to identify and monitor the collective risk potential to the business.

Within the industry the approach to risk varies for each type of organization. Many organizations, such as clearing houses, are actively involved in the risk management process. Others are operating in the markets and are controlling their risk in response to regulatory, commercial and business prudence issues and policies.

The subject of risk is a complex one and cannot easily be classified into precisely defined type or even uniform characteristics. No two risk scenarios are the same and a risk scenario will impact differently within organizations and markets.

The industry in its broadest sense has systemic risk as its highest fear. The so-called 'domino effect' of one major failure is so significant that its impact cannot be controlled and managed and it then leads to other failures which cannot be controlled until the ultimate meltdown of the financial markets and system occurs. Such a scenario does not bear thinking about and yet is it really possible it could happen?

The answer has to be yes, simply because there is in reality no way in which risk in such a globalized industry can be adequately monitored and controlled. Too many influences affect the markets in terms of trading, investment and dealing and the operational support infrastructure. How does a business manage the conflict between business opportunities and business risk? How does a firm turn away a client when it knows that other firms will accommodate that client's requirements? It is easy enough if the client expects a firm to breach regulations or laws, but if it is in the context of a type of trading or of the use or provision of a product then the decision is less easy. What are the grounds and if it is risk based, why?

Take the case of a client that is active in securities, equities and bonds, but has, to date, not made any great use of derivatives. The firm is comfortable that the client knows the markets it is trading and believes that the exposures the client takes are acceptable given the credit departments assessment of their rating etc. The client decides that it wants to make use of derivatives and so a new business opportunity exists for the firm. Does it reassess the client for suitability to trade the new product? Does the credit department revise the exposure levels it allocates for the client, and if so, how? To what extent will the firm be affected from an operations point of view if it begins trading these derivatives for the client?

These are important issues that require a balance between business risk prudence, client relationship management and operational risk control.

It may not be obvious to the firm, but the client may have been building up its expertise in derivatives and is in the process of hiring or training 'expertise'. On the other hand, the client may be worryingly naive about the requirements in terms of practical knowledge and understanding of the characteristics and trading of the products as well, of course, as being ill prepared administratively to settle such transactions.

How should the firm approach the client's request to transact derivatives? To what extent does the firm have regulatory obligations to consider? Will the client suffer from using the products and how will that reflect on the firm both in relationship terms and also in any possible legal ramifications? The pull between the desire to service the client, gain additional business and revenue and the need to ensure that there is no significant risk implication to the business is great.

The risk issues for the operations side of the firm are, of course, very different from the high-level credit and market-risk issues. It is in the areas of administrative errors, late payments and failed delivery that the risk impacts for operations. This may be linked to the problems of lack of product and market knowledge within the client, or inadequate systems to handle the products or problems meeting the disciplines and deadlines associated with the product.

We can see that there is a difference in the risk profile. On the one hand, we are concerned at the danger of the client incurring losses, possibly significant losses, in the trading of the derivatives and, on the other, the potential for problems, possibly including financial and reputation loss, caused by the inefficiency of the client in settling the transactions. The first may result in substantial financial and reputation loss and conceivably a threat to the business and the second in probably less loss but nevertheless an unwanted situation that, although unlikely to cause the demise of the firm, could still be very serious in its repercussions.

Risk is not confined to the broker/client situations, far from it. Internal risks are just as great and likely to occur more frequently. Rogue traders, fraud and unrecognized losses are massive risk issues. Not only are they potentially financially disastrous but also the implications in terms of inadequate or ineffective controls can be devastating to the future of a business. A firm that has well-publicized losses due to unrecognized trading caused by lack of adequate controls is hardly a selling point for the marketing teams! Was it a surprise that Andersen's lost clients in the immediate aftermath of their association with the Enron collapse?

Reputation and risk are so intrinsically linked that it could be argued that the reputation risk to a business is more often than not of greater significance than a financial loss. Reputation risk is naturally very evident when we look at the operations functions, as the service provided is an obvious quality benchmark. The provision of the support and settlement processes and services is not just about the efficiency in the way it is delivered and managed but also about the impact that it has on others. A client relies on the information provided by its broker, information that will be transported into systems and therefore the internal data of the broker. If that data is doubtful or, worse, corrupt it has a potentially significant impact on the client.

Not all risk is generated internally and often externally generated risk will manifest itself when the impact is already likely to be severe.

Shortage of stock in a market can lead to horrendous liquidity problems resulting in settlement fails and therefore increased risk. A firm may not be involved in this problem in the sense that it has no sales or purchases outstanding and may indeed be in a position to benefit from liquidity problems by lending stock it owns. However, should the trader or dealer sell stock short or purchase stock and then immediately sell it again there could be settlement problems and a risk that the firm could be subjected to claims etc.

Is it possible to predict risk in clearing and settlement or Operations functions? The answer is most definitely yes.

Can the risk be prevented or mitigated against? Again the answer is that in most cases yes by the simple process of introducing adequate controls and procedures supplemented by effective monitoring of the success of the controls.

Risk in financial markets is an everyday occurrence. It is fluid and can appear in more than one place and in more than one guise. Operations has a prime role in helping to control and manage the risk. However, that role is fraught with possible traps. To quote from *Against The Gods*:

> **Nothing is more soothing or more persuasive than the computer, with its imposing arrays of numbers, glowing colours and elegantly structured graphs. As we stare at the passing show, we become so absorbed that we tend to forget that the computer only answers questions; it does not ask them. When we ignore the truth, the computer supports us in our conceptual errors. Those who live only by numbers may find the computer has simply replaced the oracles to whom people resorted in ancient times for guidance in risk management and decision-making.**

With operational risk and operations risk my recommendation is trust the gut-feel and the experience of the team, not just the data from the systems.

Chapter 2

Operations and operational controls

What drives the process of the controls that the Operations teams work to? The answer is that several drivers shape the control environment for operations. Key drivers are provided by the regulatory structure of the location of the business, international regulatory conventions and market best practice. However, while these drivers are enforced by external organizations there are also major controls that are implemented and managed as corporate policy. We have issues like the risk appetite of a business that determines the extent of exposures that the business is comfortable with. We also have the internal controls environment that is established to help manage the risk appetite of the business.

Operations is a term that generically covers the processes and procedures for settlement and clearing. Therefore we have controls over those processes that are to do with the functionality of operations rather than being specific to risk. Reconciling various results of the processes is in itself a control on risk but it is equally a source of data to confirm that the process is complete. We need to be careful when we talk about controls and risk management. A control designed primarily to monitor the progress of a process or a series of processes cannot necessarily be considered to be a primary risk-management control. Likewise, a control that is designed to prevent unacceptable risk is not necessarily designed to track the progress of a process.

Within the Operations function there will be situations, processes and even procedures that create the potential for risk. Some of the situations can easily manifest themselves and would be recognized by Operations personnel. Examples of this would be workload, resource shortage, problems with key infrastructure like systems and lack of key skills sets among the personnel. In some cases the ability to introduce controls is limited and in others the effectiveness of controls can be questioned. For instance, it is neither practical nor does it make business sense to attempt to introduce controls on workload. How would you control workload, stop traders from trading? How could you introduce a control that matches resource to workload, have staff in reserve?

When we consider the workflow, infrastructure and resource within an operations team we are first and foremost looking at the ability to manage the transactions carried out by the traders or clients. There is obviously a certain fundamental requirement in terms of the data needed to perform the processes. The first control we can look at is the control over data.

Data in operations

Everything to do with the clearing, settlement and administration of transactions is dependent on data. That data can be generated externally or internally. It is utilized individually or combined with other data. It is then used either as a record or to formulate an instruction. It can be solely for the use of the organization or may be shared with others like clients or counterparties. It is received in a format and can then be transformed into a different format. Very importantly, it can be clean or corrupted.

Data is essentially what Operations is all about. Data source, data input, data interpretation and data distribution are the fundamentals of the Operations team's role today.

The control of the database and the use of data is a critical one. There are legal implications concerning the confidentiality of individuals and corporate entities. There is also the need to ensure that sensitive information for limited circulation is not distributed widely. Controls on data need to cover the following:

- Source of data
- Type of data
- Use of data

To manage this we need a policy. Below is an example of a static data policy.

This sample Static Data Policy Document is for illustrative purposes only. The content is © **The DSC.portfolio 2002**

Static data policy document

Preamble

The policy towards the sourcing, maintenance and use of static data in the business is given in this policy document. Where appropriate the policy is incorporated in the procedures manuals and has been reviewed and approved by the risk management group, internal audit and compliance.

It is important for the firm that static and variable data utilized within the business areas should be of the highest quality, should be used for the purposes it is intended for, be approved, documented, monitored, maintained and controlled in accordance with the standards set by the firm for its businesses and in compliance with any regulatory and industry practices relevant at the time.

The firm will approve the use of a central database and autonomous business area databases only if they are managed in accordance with this policy document and the procedures for the business area concerned and the firm.

Managers should note that where there is erroneous, corrupted or missing data that contributes to an error that is, or it is assumed it will be, deemed to be ***market***, ***credit or operational risk*** (e.g. financial, regulatory, reputational) there are specific procedures given in this document for reporting the situation immediately to the Database Manager and the Risk Management Group (RMG).

Managers should note, and make their staff aware of, the restrictions on the use of certain static data and in particular that which relates to clients and which may be subject to commercial confidentiality issues, 'Chinese Walls' or Client Data Protection.

If there is any doubt about the use of the information the legal department must be consulted and approval given by them for the use of the data.

Policy guideline

Guidelines are provided for the following types of data:

1. Exchanges and Clearing Houses
2. Products (Exchange Traded)
3. Products (OTC)
4. Company Data
5. Market Data (Trading and Economic)
6. Prices
7. Clearing and Settlement Data
8. Corporate Actions
9. Client Data
10. Finance and Accounting
11. Banking and Payment Data
12. Regulatory and Compliance
13. Reporting and M.I.

14 Risk
15 System Data
16 H.R. and Payroll
17 Other

Guidelines are provided for the following processes in the Central Data Control Department (CDCD):

1 Data Requirement
2 Data Sourcing
3 Data Maintenance
4 Data Use

Data requirement

Each operational area must provide CDCD with their data requirement. CDCD will require and maintain a record of:

- The type of data required to be held
- Reason for the data being held
- Whether the data is for internal and or external use
- Who is responsible for approving the data requirement
- The cost of obtaining and using the data

Data sourcing

CDCD will, in conjunction with the managers, source data. CDCD will maintain a record of the approved sources of data, monitor them for quality and make additions/deletions to sources of data as appropriate. CDCD will advise business areas of changes and will maintain the following records on-line for reference:

- The source or sources for the data required
- How the source of data is benchmarked for accuracy and completeness

- The results of the benchmarking
- Adjustments to data sources
- Mandatory sources of data
- Non-mandatory sources of data (see Business Area Database)

In the above sample we can see how the controls over data are built up by addressing the three points of source, type and use. The more complex the structure and the business of a firm, the greater the data management issue and the greater the operations and operational risk to the organization

Controls over data are important but so to is the control over systems and people. This can be linked to data or standalone.

People and system controls

The management of people and systems is a key function of the managers and supervisors. The objectives are:

- Risk management
- Efficiency
- Cost effectiveness
- Competitive advantage
- Developing and implementing procedures
- Control
- Compliance with regulation and controls
- Business development
- Continuity and development of staff
- Provision of client services
- Record keeping

The demands on managers and supervisors are considerable. Today the role has been expanded and as well as operational issues such as processes and procedures, we now have skills requirements in the client-facing and risk-management areas. We can also add to this an involvement in profit generation and protection.

With such a change in the role and a situation where significant change is also occurring in the industry in all sorts of ways, the manager's role in ensuring that systems are capable of handling the current and future business and that the team is being trained and retrained to meet the new environment, is, to say the least, demanding.

Managing systems

Systems are crucial to operations. The effectiveness of systems depends on both the suitability of the system for the business being undertaken and the capability of managers and supervisors to utilize the system. It is also essential that the systems are recognized as key risk components being vulnerable to both failure and security risk.

The interaction between people and systems is at the heart of the operations function. Links to various sources of information as well as users accessing the systems will be a key factor in the effectiveness and efficiency of the operation in general and impacts significantly in areas such as:

- Client-facing products and services
- Group Risk Management
- STP projects

The robustness of systems is a key regulatory requirement, it is also a key internal risk matter. One only needs to look at cases where system failures have precipitated dire consequences for organizations. Brokerage businesses have ceased functioning because of the inability to meet the regulatory competency levels for settlement of transactions. Failures in control over static data, system access and input and amendment of data have generated high-profile 'disasters'.

Consider the following extract from the Futures and Options Association (FOA) Guidelines for End-users of Derivatives published in 1995 yet still a fundamental concept today.

Insight

Systems Approval

Computer systems used for recording derivative transactions should be subject to the same procedures and controls as for other systems used by the organization (including contingency plans and back-up). In particular, the pricing models and trade recording systems should be properly controlled to ensure that only authorized amendments or overrides are made. Derivative systems should be reviewed to ensure that they integrate properly into the organization's normal reporting systems, that they are sufficiently robust to be able to continue to operate as the number of transactions increases and that they comply with any applicable regulatory requirements.

In short there is a specific need with various products to have both adequate systems and controls in place over the use of those systems such that the data and the system itself cannot be manipulated.

However, as systems are linked to enable the processing of transactions, settlements, payments etc. as well as providing data to management information systems, the control over access, input, static data, distribution, etc. is no small task.

Figure 2.1 shows some of the generic links between systems. It is obvious that many processes and instructions move between these systems every day. All this data is critical and the robustness factor means that no weak link can exist in the chain without serious implications for quality, reliability and risk control.

Given this importance of the systems, which cannot be overemphasized, there are significant questions for managers to answer:

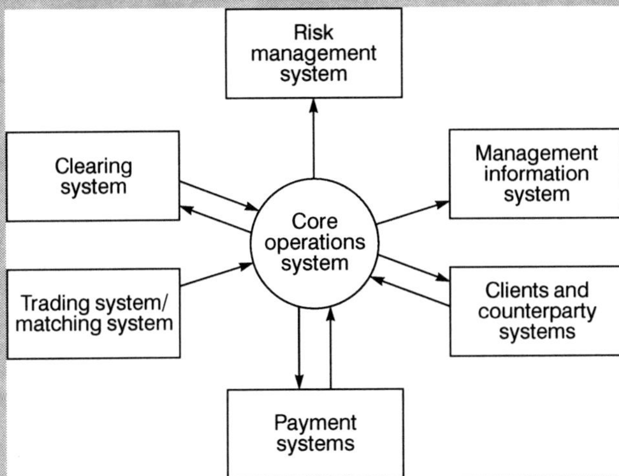

Figure 2.1 Generic links between systems

- What are the objectives for the systems employed?
- How is the effectiveness of systems measured?
- What are the resource and skill sets needed for support?
- What are the contingency plans that are needed against failures?
- What level and type of security policy is needed for the systems?
- What are the benefits and disadvantages of the systems used?
- What integration and interaction with other internal/external systems will occur?

Each of these questions must be answered if managers and supervisors are to be in control of the systems used in the operations area. In measuring the system performance we first need to differentiate between the technical performance and the operational performance.

Technical performance

Policy on which system supplier, operating platform, etc. will normally be a decision that rests with a central IT function.

Operations managers will naturally be involved in the deliberations. The IT area will decide whether the system is performing to the specifications required and will update, upgrade and maintain the systems

Operational performance

This involves the Operations managers and supervisors monitoring the performance of the system in relation to the original objectives. Technical issues will come into this process as system downtime etc. will be logged and raised with the technical support team.

Other performance issues will be the ability of the system to:

- Generate the data in the required format
- Timely production of data
- Handle products
- Complete functions such as margin and revaluation
- Interface with other systems
- Security

To be able to undertake this performance-monitoring requirement, data will be required from:

- The system itself
- Evaluation data from users

In both cases logs need to be maintained and received. This data must then be analysed to provide a continuous profile of the system from both technical and operational viewpoints. The analysis will concentrate on the impact of the system's performance on the workflow. The combination of the data and analysis of impact will permit the managers to monitor developments of new software and/ or upgrading and replacement of systems. As changes, and in particular a switch to a new system, is not something that can be achieved at the drop of a hat, the monitoring of system performance, and its impact, is vitally important in terms of controls.

In respect of contingency planning, without a clear understanding of the systems role, and the duration of each task in the process we cannot prioritize the processes in the event of any kind of system failure or problem. This subject is looked at again later in the book.

Security over data on systems is also a key issue. Logging on to the system needs to be monitored and verified as authorized. Password discipline needs to be enforced through education of its importance and effective controls.

People and performance management

The performance of people is driven by their own motivation and that provided by their supervisors and managers. It is an important aspect of the general controls over an Operations function that people are recognized as a key element as well as a potential source of risk.

Measuring that performance of teams and people is essential in the process of maintaining standards but is also potentially one of the most difficult tasks performed by the manager/supervisor. Traditional forms of performance measurement such as appraisals have merit provided they are done well. If they are not done well the outcome is usually a major disaster. Most people believe they are doing well, some believe they are performing impressively. To be told otherwise is not easy to take even when deep down the person concerned knows the facts to be true. It is important to be aware that the supervisor and manager have very different roles in the team. Both are motivators and organizers (in different ways) and both sit in judgment on the individuals and the team.

That judgment and the individual's expectations are frequently at odds with each other and as a result relationships, performance (individual and the team) and the working environment can dramatically change for the worse. This reduces the efficiency and increases the risk but how is this problem overcome?

The controls over personnel are about capability in respect of the tasks and the function as well as the personal wellbeing and development of the individual. Controls to make sure processes are resourced by people experienced enough to undertake the task must be supplemented by controls to ensure that working environment, training and development are all properly managed and implemented. It is important to recognize here that there are employment law issues to consider and controls must be devised that ensure compliance with requirements.

Performance measurement

Managers and supervisors will have a feel for how their team is performing and that 'feel' is an essential benchmark.

However, there needs to be more substance to the analysis of performance if it is to be part of risk controls and this takes the form of comparisons, tracking and adjustments to procedures.

Analysis of workflow, through the use of workflow charts for instance, will achieve two things:

- Provide the data needed to make any adjustment to structure and or procedures
- Show team members that management is aware of the current and potential future situations

Accurate management information on performance of individuals, the team, the procedures and the controls is vital for any realistic and therefore meaningful assessments to be made. There is a danger that staff will interpret workflow analysis as having hidden agendas like headcount reduction. Adequate involvement and communication will overcome this, particularly if the positive outcome of the process is explained.

Workflow analysis in generic terms provides data on:

- What is being processed and when
- How it is impacted by factors such as volume
- What resource is available
- Where pressure points are
- Where problems are or may occur
- What scope there is for change

By analysing the primary, secondary and periodic processes and tasks, their expected and actual duration and whether the resource is being optimized the managers can judge the performance level. They can also plan ahead, introduce change and have information to support their argument for change.

These charts are simple to produce and maintain and provide credible support information essential to the day-to-day and long-term management of the operations team. This is also a fundamental part of risk mapping and management as we see later in the book.

Management of people

If we want to put this whole subject into perspective we need to draw together the issues outlined above and consider how these interact. We also need to consider any suitable external benchmarks etc. that help to assess the controls.

Figure 2.2 gives some ideas on this subject. This figure attempts to show how the source of information and analysis is utilized to provide various viewpoints on the assessment of systems and people and the controls being employed. This will enable managers to

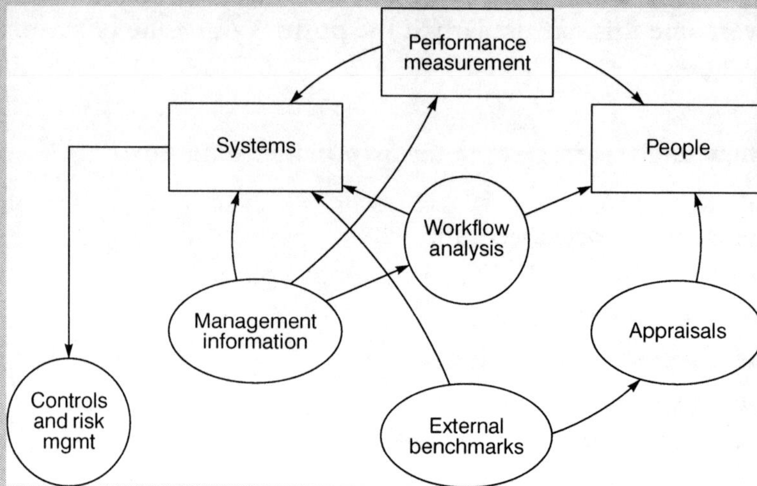

Figure 2.2 Assessment of systems and the controls deployed

make informed decisions on everything from salaries and grades to system enhancement and procedure changes. What can be seen is the complexity of the information flow and how each flow interacts with another flow before finally enabling the system to generate data for controls and risk management use. In many cases the information is routinely available while in others it may need research, like external benchmarks. Once it is obtained a whole range of options are available all of which help in managing people and system processes.

A few examples would be:

- Training requirements
- System enhancements
- Automation
- Better working environment
- Contingency planning
- Business planning
- Motivation

This in turn enables effective controls to be developed that monitor data, people and processes.

Summary

Managing data, people and systems is not something to be taken lightly, the risk in doing so is too great. Communication and awareness are essential, respect must be earned and that can only be achieved with adequate information gleaned from sources such as controls reviews, appraisals, management information, workflow charts, etc.

Underestimating the complexity of the task of developing and, importantly, maintaining controls would be foolish.

Chapter 3

An introduction to operations and operational risk

The subject of risk raises several key issues. These include:

- The approach to risk
- The sources of risk
- The impact of risk
- Measuring risk including the cost of managing risk
- Introducing controls and procedures
- Why disasters will happen if it is not managed

Operational risk and operations risk are not new. As soon as the first trade took place operational risk came into being and yet it is only comparatively recently that there has been an acceptance that operational risk exists. Contrast this with market and credit risk both of which have been recognized since the 1970s.

Market and credit risk

Definition

Market risk can be simply described as the risk of financial loss due to trading errors, liquidity issues, adverse market movements or breaches of market rules and regulations.
Credit risk can be simply described as the risk of financial loss due to the likelihood of a failure by a counterparty. This loss can be failure to receive either cash or assets or both and the cost or replacement.

Both market and credit risk have been high on the agenda of regulators and risk managers. An example is perhaps the capital adequacy requirements pertaining to over-the-counter derivative transactions and now operational risk itself. Risk in the financial markets needs to be managed not to prevent people making losses on their activities, that is part of their business, but to prevent the losses being so great and so concentrated that they create the 'domino' effect; a collapse of the whole industry. Another term used to describe this kind of scenario is systemic risk and we will return to this concept in terms of Operations later in the book.

For a considerable period of time the only likely source of such a catastrophe was considered to be either market problems or problems with a counterparty not honouring their obligations. Today there is a realization that other factors can play a prominent part in risk and that operational risk is one of those factors.

Operational risk

We saw in Chapter 1 the definition of operational risk according to the Basel Committee, but are there other definitions of operational risk? The answer is yes. Many organizations recognize the Basel definition but also have internal definitions of what constitutes operational risk. One reason for the delay in recognizing operational risk as a category of risk is probably the difficulty many organizations face in determining what exactly operational risk is!

Some would argue that it is everything that affects a business that is not market or credit risk. Others argue that it is everything and anything to do with the post-transaction clearing and settlement process. In the case of the latter the risk itself is described as 'operations' rather than operational risk.

For the purposes of this book we will consider both operational and operations risk not least because they are very much linked. To analyse operational risk we need to understand the approach to risk that the various participants in the industry take. This approach depends on the type of transactions undertaken and the nature of the business concerned. The regulatory environment that the organization operates under will also determine the approach adopted.

Another key factor is that many view the subject of risk primarily in terms of potential financial loss. As such, operations risk is frequently considered to be unlikely to cause a severe financial loss and certainly not in one hit. The logic here is that an inappropriate or incorrect deal can result in substantial loss whereas a settlement problem with the transaction, while it may incur costs, is not likely to generate a significant loss.

One is tempted initially to agree with these sentiments as history would tend to suggest that the headline-making 'disasters' in the financial services industry are all mainly related to market and/or credit risk in the sense that they involve significant positions in securities and derivatives where the obligations could not be met. However, delve a little deeper and there may be associated operations issues that contributed to the problem. The contribution may not have been 'physical' in the sense of an error in processing transactions but rather a failure to carry out the risk management role, for instance reconciliation, that Operations team undoubtedly have.

Manifestation of operational risk

Operational, as distinct from operations, risk can manifest itself in many ways. Sometimes the operational risk will be such that it is not easily or immediately identifiable. In most cases an error on a transaction can and should be identified quickly and adjusted so that the loss is quantified. Within operations, for instance, a problem may be occurring only occasionally and yet is having an unseen, dramatic and damaging effect. For instance, a client is being inconvenienced and as a result is losing confidence in their broker/bank as their counterparty. In such a situation it is not inconceivable that the client may gradually move their business elsewhere and the counterparty may never be aware that it is the Operations team's performance that is to blame.

So is that operational or operations risk? The answer is both. Operational risk because the business has been unable to run efficiently and has lost a client and revenue. In all probability others will move their business elsewhere if the problems occur and so financial and reputation loss arise. Operations risk because it is a lack of skills that is creating errors and lack of controls that is failing to prevent the errors impacting. In Figure 3.1 the operational risk had its origins in the operations area and concluded as an operational risk of the haemorrhaging of clients, revenue and reputation.

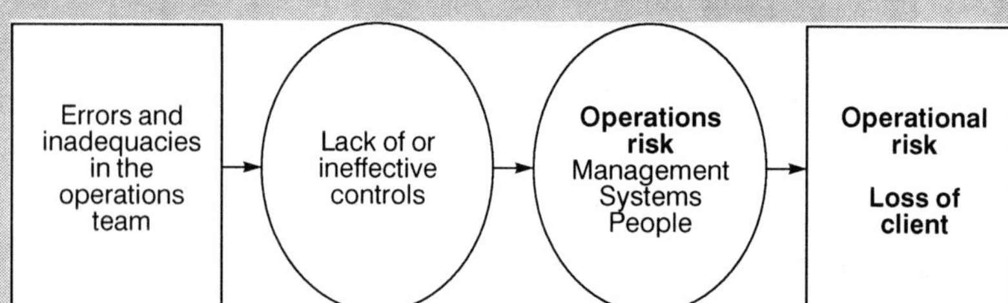

Figure 3.1 The origins of operational risk

Operational risk could also be generated in IT, internal audit, compliance, accounting and premises. In fact anything that curtails, disrupts or has a negative impact on a business is operational risk. Elevators not working might have a minor impact that is more of an inconvenience than a risk, but that becomes a greater risk if it is a twenty-storey tower and you are on the top floor. However, a transport strike might have a more extensive impact and a fire in the building would make it impossible to continue business unless there is a disaster recovery plan and site to move to.

The importance of disaster recovery (DR) was graphically illustrated by the dreadful atrocities of 11 September 2001 when terrorists attacked the World Trade Center in New York. The collapse of the twin towers obviously destroyed numerous businesses and their normal infrastructure. The ability to move to a DR site became crucial. Some moved to ready-prepared sites, others to hotel rooms. However, the real operational risk was not the loss of the towers, terrible and difficult as that was, but the tragedy of the loss of people. In DR terms buildings, systems, records and equipment can be replaced, often reasonably easily. People cannot.

The enormity of the impact on relatives, colleagues and loved ones of the loss of life on that terrible day was greater than any business consideration and yet it does now, months later, show us how much of an operational risk the loss of many employees at the same time can be. So operational risk ranges from the impact of other risks like operations risk to the potential, but hopefully less frequent risk of massive disruption through loss of infrastructure and resource.

Operations risk

In simplistic terms operations risk is all about what happens within the business areas defined as administrative, trading support and record keeping, etc. As such, settlement risk is probably the key risk but other types of risk, particularly system risk, are just as significant. Operations teams and managers are obviously in the front line in terms of risk management when we are looking at operations risk, but they also have a significant role in operational risk management. Table 3.1 shows some of the areas of Operations or issues that can be included as potential for operations risk.

We can see from this short list that the risk itself is likely to be very different depending on its source but, most importantly, we can see how a risk situation in one area can affect another. For example, a system failure could delay reconciliation which in turn causes a

Table 3.1 Areas of potential operations risk

Trade capture	Controls
Money laundering and fraud	Custody
Personnel	Cash management
Settlement	Asset management
Systems	Reconciliation
External counterparties	Procedures

settlement fail. This is an example of the 'systemic' risk mentioned earlier, one risk starts a train of risks and the impact almost certainly grows in severity. We look at operations risk in detail in the next chapter.

Quantifying and measuring operational risk

Operational risk is a question of identifying the source, which can be difficult. It is also difficult to measure and hard to quantify in terms of likely financial loss. It is therefore not easy to allocate capital to cover such a risk turning into an actual loss.

The establishing of the extent of the market risk associated with trading is not simple but it is nevertheless possible to measure the exposure given various scenarios and to allocate capital to cover the possible worst-case outcome. Value-at-Risk (VaR) is one common approach but it is less easy to apply this when dealing with operational risk.

Nevertheless, progress is being made on operational risk models as more and more organizations seek to quantify the operational risk of their business. It is therefore important that managers begin the process of measuring risk by developing risk – measurement models suitable for in-house use.

The Basel Committee have published consultative papers on operational risk details of which are available from their website (see Appendix 1) and these should be studied to understand how the thinking on operational risk has evolved.

General risk measurement of operational and operations risk

On a day-to-day basis when we look at quantifying and measuring operations and operational risk we need to first consider what it consists of. At high level, operational risk can be said to comprise two types of risk:

- Operations risk
- Non-operations risk

Operations risk is any or all of:

- Settlement risk
- System risk
- Personnel risk
- Infrastructure risk
- Counterparty risk
- Regulatory risk
- Legal risk
- Reputational risk

Non-operations risk is any or all of:

- Systemic risk (firm and industry)
- Management risk
- Infrastructure risk
- Counterparty risk
- Regulatory risk
- Legal risk

- Reputational risk
- Political risk
- Controls failure

However, within these headings are many subsets of risk that can and often do combine to generate risk situations that go across one or more categories. We will look at these operations and non-operations risks in detail in a later chapter.

Combinations of risk

The combination of risks makes measuring and managing operational risk a complex exercise and indeed it can also result in the situation where the cost of managing the risk is prohibitive.

As with all types of risk, there is operational risk that is acceptable as part of the business provided that the risk is known and understood. There is a danger that the subject of operational risk can be so diverse and so large that it becomes an administrative and costly nightmare. It is therefore important for any organization and any individual manager with responsibility for operational risk to establish exactly what the objectives are when we talk about measuring and managing operational risk.

One question, however, probably keeps on coming to mind.

What is risk?

Consider the following ten statements about risk. Each has a observation or comment about risk and will help us to decide what our view of risk is and therefore what our approach to risk management will be.

1 Operational risk exists in all businesses
2 We can ascertain what operational risk is in the context of our business
3 We can look at individual components of the risk
4 We can choose:
   4.1 To be aware of the risk
   4.2 To be aware of the risk and prioritize managing some of it
   4.3 To manage the risk out of the business
5 We may need to adopt a mix and match approach
6 We may need to demonstrate how we manage operational risk:
   6.1 To clients or potential clients
   6.2 To third parties such as clearing houses
   6.3 To regulators
7 We will have to establish a risk culture within the organization
8 We need to analyse risk in conjunction with
   8.1 Other parts of the organization
   8.2 External counterparties
   8.3 Across products and markets
9 We will need to allocate capital to mitigate the impact of the operational risk manifesting itself and totally ignoring operational risk is not an option
10 We will need structured risk management procedures

These statements about risk show us the way in which an organization will need to construct a risk policy, in fact several risk policies under a general one to reflect different aspects of the business like trading, fund management, operations, custody, etc. From that will come the designing of controls, procedures and risk management processes that the business needs.

One important issue is the ability to demonstrate the rationale behind risk assumptions, the way in which the impact of the risk is assessed and what mitigates the risk actually occurring. Comprehensive, mathematical risk models are extensively used in managing market and credit risk. This book will not go into those but instead will look at the rather crude models that can be used quite effectively in the operations area on a day-to-day basis.

Operational and operations risk models

We need to be able to measure risk in such a way that we can predict:

- The type of risk
- Where, when and how it will arise
- The frequency with which it might occur
- The impact

There are a variety of ways in which this can be done and we will look at risk measuring a little later.

What are the objectives of modelling the risk? BIS offer different ways of assessing operational risk and this is a useful guide to (a) how we have to approach risk from a regulatory point of view and (b) how we may want to approach it for internal control purposes.

Operations risk modelling can be a process of assessing weaknesses and strengths in the overall procedures and processes carried out in the function. One example of assessment is by carrying out a process of workflow analysis that will show, among other things:

- The processes and their duration
- The complexity, ranking (in terms of primary, secondary) and the extent of automation of these processes
- The deadlines associated with the processes
- The level of resource available for the process
- The level of management needed
- The scope to absorb additional workload and or delays to the processing

Workflow analysis

Workflow analysis is discussed later in the chapter but from the above we can see that some kind of operations and operational risk measurement are both possible. It must be noted that this can initially be a time-consuming process and, once undertaken, this will become a continuous process if it is to have any meaningful impact. It is also a different kind of analysis, although with much in common with that which is probably being done anyway by supervisors. Is it worth it?

Look at it like this. We can choose not to measure, even crudely, the risk on the basis that it may never create a major problem but then you could leave your house unlocked all day and never get burgled!

Having established that operations and operational risk exist and need to be quantified and measured, we need to identify the risk in more detail. We will do this later but first let us look at where the risk might come from.

Sources of operational risk

Here are just a few potential sources:

- Lack of product knowledge
- Poor system reliability
- Inadequate levels of staffing
- Inefficient counterparties
- Diverse and unpredictable business levels
- Overseas clients
- Lack of critical skill sets
- Fraud and criminal activity
- Poor communication and poor internal relationships

Quite how the source of risk occurs or what the implications are will vary and this is perhaps one of the most difficult things to incorporate into analysis of risk. When does an error that is likely to be a natural occurrence as part of the processes used in the operations environment become a significant risk issue?

Take lack of product knowledge, for instance. What is the level of product knowledge that removes risk from the equation? When does someone know it all? When does a team of people know it all? Do we need to be experts on everything to do with a product or just about the material things that affect our ability to settle that trade?

Type and frequency of risk

Each of the sources shown above is very different and so are the types of risk and the frequency with which they might occur. Continuing to use product knowledge as the example, lack of product knowledge could be as a result of:

- Turnover of staff
- Loss of experienced personnel
- New products being traded
- Non-availability or difficulty in obtaining information
- Lack of training

It may be a major problem or it may only be relevant if and when a particular type of product is traded. Bear in mind also that other risks may become associated such as regulatory risk and reputational risk.

For example, a clearing member will usually have to demonstrate to the clearing house the competency of the staff, systems and processes. If problems occur at the member because of the introduction of a new type of product the clearing house may feel that the member is failing to meet the standards required. Any prolonged problem or subsequent repetition of problems with settlement or meeting the clearing house procedures may result in the clearing status being withdrawn.

Another example is that a problem might manifest itself as an error because we were not aware of something like a corporate action, a derivative expiry date or because we were unaware of problems with settlement in the jurisdiction where the product was traded.

Some of the problems may be quite obvious, others more obscure. Individually the problem might be easily identified and managed but a combination of risk problems might create a far more difficult situation to manage. The role of Operations in managing risk is therefore very important.

Chapter 4

The role of Operations in managing risk

We have already seen that much of what we do in an operational environment or an Operations team, day in day out, is geared to directly or indirectly managing risk. A major issue that arises is that the personnel involved in the Operations team may not be aware of it. Perversely that in itself is a source of risk!

Summarizing operations and operational risk

It is a combination of types and sources of risk that may have a different impact in various circumstances. It may result in direct or indirect financial loss. It may occur frequently or occasionally. It may build up gradually until it is a major problem. It is a risk category of immense importance and must be understood in any organization, large or small. It is hard to measure but nevertheless must be addressed so that, at the very least, managers are aware of the risks. Failure to understand and address operational risk will result in significant damage to the business.

Types of operations risk

In the previous chapter we considered the fact that risk comes in a variety of guises and that we can break down risk into several headings. Within each heading will be a complex matrix of possibilities and sources of the risk type. Let us try to define some of the types of risk.

Settlement risk

Definition

The risk of inefficient processes and procedures resulting in the failure, delay or incorrect settlement of transactions and associated actions such as payments, delivery and corporate actions.

There are many ways in which this type of risk can occur. The simple inefficiencies of the staff involved are an obvious source. So too is inadequate or misused systems. However, not all settlement risk is created within the operations team. External influences such as delays in getting relevant information from front office to operations or problems with systems run on a bureau basis can be very influential.

Other possible causes of settlement risk are:

- Client transactions
- Deadlines
- Difficult settlement conventions
- Illiquid stocks/bonds/commodities
- Lack of knowledge of the product/processes/procedures associated with the transaction

System risk

Definition

The failure or absence of adequate systems to handle the type of business being transacted and security over such systems.

The reliance on systems in the financial services industry makes system risk a key issue. Key processes rely on systems and many current and major projects involve technology (for example, straight through processing (STP)). The advent of straight through processing is removing elements of settlement risk associated with trade input. Electronic markets, internal dealing systems and direct trade input enable the operations team to maximize auto reconciliation and concentrate on exception management. Linking this then into automated clearing systems and client-facing systems, together with reporting and risk management, completes the STP path.

However, not all organizations have straight through processing, or if they do it is not necessarily fully front to back. Whatever the situation, the managers must recognize that systems generate considerable capacity, provide efficient and cost-effective processing **and** those systems are also a major source of operational risk.

Another massive system risk issue is system security. The security over the system is paramount. All too often there are serious problems generated by the failure of managers to manage systems adequately. There are a whole host of possible situations including:

- Incorrect, missing or erroneously changed static data
- Failure to make changes to static data
- Ignored, lack of or breached security of access to the system or parts of the system
- 'Shared' passwords leading to breach of segregation
- Access to confidential client information gained by the front office
- Inadequate or absence of monitoring of client-facing technology services
- Lack of or easily breached firewalls
- Lack or absence of control over access to the Internet
- Private, illegal or unauthorized access, download, etc.
- Possibility of hackers and/or viruses entering the system

We also need to consider system capability and reliability. In terms of capability it is fairly obvious that any system or systems used in an operations area needs to be able to handle adequately the products traded. Where this is not possible as might be the case with use of, say, over-the-counter derivatives, controls need to be devised which will mitigate the risk. Client or end-user organizations can have problems with systems capabilities, for instance in verifying margin calls from a CCP. If this is the case with the systems they use, managers need to address this issue with suitable controls encompassing the reasonableness of the data supplied to them by the brokers.

The issue about reliability hardly needs any explanation. In terms of reliability, there needs to be awareness of the manual process that can/will be implemented in the event of a problem with availability of the system or its ability to handle a product or process. We also need to consider the impact this will have on the risk exposure, what procedures and controls will now apply and what the potential solutions there are to eradicate the unreliability.

Counterparty risk

Definition

Counterparty risk is not confined to creditworthiness. The poor settlement performance of a counterparty, be it a client, an exchange, a clearing house, custodian or agent, can have a material effect on the broker's Operations team, causing an increase in errors, delayed settlement and the funding of obligations leading to a higher level of risk.

In most organizations there are numerous relationships with external parties such as agents, clients and exchange/clearing houses. Very often the relationship is a prime source of critical information on trading and settlement.

Where it is necessary to use an agent, for instance an institutional client using a broker or a broker/bank using a clearing agent on an exchange where they do not have clearing membership, there is potential for heightened operational risk. The standards of performance by these agents will inevitably impact upon the processes and performance of our own team. Late settlement, notification, or payment are all significant risk issues and may have far-reaching implications. Some issues that arise are related to regulatory, reputation, client money and assets segregation, increased costs and administration through claims for failed or late settlement, etc.

Clients create similar kinds of issues. A broker is dependent on the accurate and timely flow of information concerning transactions, payments, booking instructions, etc. If a position is to go to delivery on settlement date the broker/bank is dependent on the client meeting the delivery schedule and deadlines or, in a CCP situation, they become liable themselves.

In some cases there may be very limited resource and product knowledge at the client and the potential for problems is increased. In many cases the broker/bank may also be dealing with a custodian. One perceived way of reducing the risk of problems with clients is to offer them a range of client services designed to help them in the processes.

Brokers, banks and custodians offer a wide range of client services including global clearing, single-currency settlement, average pricing and total packages like prime brokerage.

While potentially of great value in reducing the risk at the client, each of these is placing additional pressures on the operations processing flow and therefore while it can be said that client services help to reduce counterparty risk (by providing vital assistance to smooth the settlement flow) its provision does create additional sources of risk internally.

Personnel risk

Definition

The risk of a member or members of staff creating an adverse risk situation for the Operations team, or the inability to manage the personnel situation in an Operations team.

Key issues that arise under this source of risk include:

- Fraud
- Defections/loss of key or senior staff
- Lack of contingency for absence of staff
- Inadequate training and development
- Relationship issues (work and private)
- Excessive pressure caused by poor working environment and hours

The issue of personnel risk is often ignored and yet the efficiency and effectiveness of the operations team, which is key to profitability and competitiveness, is directly related to the manager's ability to develop the right people and the right environment, which in turn is at the heart of risk management.

One fundamental risk control is to establish a risk culture within the operations team. Lack of attention to personnel risk will, sooner or later, create a major problem, as other risk control measures are dependent upon and assume a 'risk culture' has been established in the team.

Regulatory risk

Definition

The risk of financial and reputation loss created by breaches of regulations and failure to adequately enforce compliance with rules and standards of regulators and other organizations.

It is often tempting to ignore regulatory risk on the misguided assumption that compliance and or audit will protect against any problem. Recognizing regulatory risk as part of operations and operational risk is essential simply because the consequences of not doing so is too great. Regulatory risk stems from several sources including:

- Reporting requirements
- Client money rules
- Money laundering and fraud (insider dealing)
- Complex and differing requirements in regulatory jurisdictions
- Reputational impact of a publicly reported breach of regulation and punitive action

The role of Operations in countering regulatory risk is to be aware of the regulatory requirements and to have effective communication with compliance and audit. Too often both audit and compliance are viewed in a negative light by personnel. As part of the creation of a risk culture the managers must reverse this view.

Legal risk

Definition

The risk of being unable to obtain settlement or ownership of assets, to receive cash due, or to enforce agreements and documentation with counterparties resulting in irrecoverable loss. It is also being in breach of the laws applicable in different jurisdictions where the business may carry on activities.

As with regulation, it is tempting to say that legal issues are dealt with elsewhere in the organization. However, there are many instances where operations personnel are either directly or indirectly involved with matters that present a risk.

These will include the ineffective, absence of or incorrect client documentation in respect of transactions undertaken, the seizing or impounding of assets and entering into illegal transactions or relationships or carrying out actions/instructions that would be considered illegal in the UK or elsewhere that activity is undertaken.

Just as with regulation, there needs to be awareness of potential legal issues and good communication with the legal departments and advisers.

Financial risk

Definition

The risk of financial loss caused by unnecessary errors, incorrect processes, inadequate or missing procedures or unauthorized actions including instructions, payments and transfer of assets.

Some elements of financial risk could be classified as settlement risk. This might include errors resulting in interest claims or fines for late delivery, for instance. However, financial risk does exist in other forms as part operations and operational risk. Included in this would be:

- Fraud
- Defaulting on obligations
- Ineffective costs management
- Unclaimed and or unreconciled income such as dividends and interest
- Poor treasury management

These are risks often 'lost' in the overall process of running an Operations team. Costs management, for instance, may be an issue when business is slow but is relaxed when revenues and profits are good.

Likewise, significant additional costs or underperformance of returns on invested capital occur if treasury management is neglected or is carried out by inadequately trained personnel. It may not be noticeable on a day-by-day basis but the cumulative effect over a year can be very significant.

Disaster risk

Definition

This broadly constitutes the inability, or reduced ability to continue to operate and can cover such areas as inadequate disaster recovery or business-continuation plans, the forcing of a curtailment or reduction in trading levels and allowing unacceptable risk situations to occur.

Many organizations have adequate contingency plans for disasters such as loss of premises. From an operations point of view there are many possible disaster situations that have nothing to do with the loss of premises. Some of these would be:

- Sudden unavailability of staff
- Prolonged system downtime
- External factors such as problems at agents, clearing houses, clients
- Breaches of client confidentiality
- Unauthorized use of assets
- Failure of controls

Summary

In this chapter we have given an overview of the role of Operations in risk. We have considered what it is, where it comes from and how it occurs.

We have looked at simplistic ways in which this risk can be defined and at some of the key issues that will need to be managed. In the next chapter we consider mapping the risks and the controls that need to be in place in the Operations function.

Operations and operational risk is a vital element that needs to be considered by any business operating in the financial markets. It is a large and diverse subject that needs careful assessment, interpretation of its characteristics in relation to each organization and, above all, managing. We can therefore conclude that the manager's role in operational risk management is a crucial one.

Chapter 5

Developing controls

Risk in an Operations environment

Understanding the risk sources and the impact of that risk requires a process called risk mapping. This essentially involves the analysis of the workflow and the critical tasks through the clearing and settlement process. It is also prudent to consider any risk sources that occur pre-clearing and settlement as these form part of operational risk and may also contribute to credit and or market risk management processes. These would include pre-trade checks on:

- Authorized products
- Deal limits
- Position and exposure limits
- Counterparty limits
- Liquidity limits

Other areas in the organization such as credit and compliance will monitor some of these. However, the Operations area is involved in some of this process as the information produced on, for instance, positions is critical to the accurate risk management process for positions and other limits.

The risk cycle, as Figure 5.1 shows, is a continuous process. It does not take holidays and it can occur however busy or quiet a business might be. Controls must recognize this and be able to address risk 24 hours a day, 365 days a year.

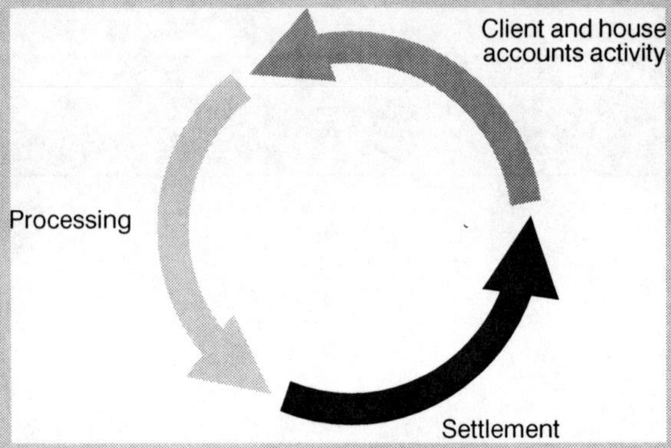

Figure 5.1 The risk cycle. (*Source*: Computer Based Learning Ltd)

Key functions such as reconciliation and error resolution must be effective otherwise the dealing function is hampered and/or the organization is put at risk by 'hidden' positions, unauthorized exposures, etc. As these will present not only an unacceptable risk but also a breach of regulation the consequences are clear.

The process of mapping risk takes into account the workflow in generic and then in segmented form dealing with key tasks and functions. Tasks are also ranked by how critical they are in the settlement and other processes.

Critical task high-level analysis

Here we will try to define the key tasks that form the core element of the operations function. This process will enable us to understand the activity and the impact that certain events have on the processes. In turn this enables us to develop effective controls and procedures.

Below are some examples of critical core tasks, their characteristics and key elements of the task

Trade input

Characteristics:

Can be manual or automated or a combination of both

Key elements of the process:

- Source of trade data
- Deal ticket processing
- Format considerations in terms of duration of task
- Volume
- Peaks and troughs, influencing issues like economic announcements etc.
- Allocation of trade or account bookings

Trade input is increasingly an automated process driven from a dealing system. However, where there is still a manual process of re-keying data there will need to be controls to cover the method and frequency of receipt of trade data, i.e. deal tickets collected from a designated point at regular intervals.

Valuation

Characteristics:

Control process that values the transaction for settlement, margin, collateral and profit/loss calculations

Key elements of the process

- Sources of prices
- Input method – manual/automatic
- Validation of prices

- Generation of profit/loss figures
- Valuing collateral
- Portfolio reporting
- Frequency of valuation

Valuation is a key process and also a control function. Price source is an issue in terms of both reliability and availability. Some organizations use two sources of prices to ensure the credibility of data produced as a result of the valuation. For instance, a fund can have real problems if the valuation of the assets is significantly incorrect. Valuation of collateral is also a crucial control process as the collateral is an insurance against possible risk.

In many cases the problems with valuations stems from deadlines and completeness of the positions being valued as well as from the accuracy and availability of the price information. Non-exchange-traded (unlisted) securities, OTC derivatives and illiquid securities can all present pricing problems and adequate procedures and controls are needed.

Settlement and corporate actions

Characteristics:

The process of exchanging assets and cash for other assets or cash in final conclusion of a transaction by establishing a change of ownership of the assets or cash and then to manage any benefits that occur by way of ownership of the cash or assets.

Key elements of the process

- Trade matching and confirmation
- Settlement instructions

- Asset delivery
- Cash availability
- Dealing with settlement fails
  - Claims
  - Stock borrowing
  - Repos
  - Buy-ins
  - Partial settlement
  - Managing settlement queues
- Managing corporate actions
  - Obtaining data on corporate actions
  - Dealing with corporate actions
  - Claiming benefits
  - Managing actions on loaned and borrowing stock

The central processes in settlement can be diverse, are not uniform and utilize information from many sources, therefore controls over the various elements of the process must be comprehensive, workable and continually monitored for effectiveness. They will need to cover areas such as problem identification, timetables for action and escalation procedures, resolution options, etc. As volumes of business will fluctuate and certain transactions may have or need to have priority for settlement controls must be relevant to the product and the settlement convention of that product.

Corporate actions are mandatory or voluntary, sometimes have elements of both, and errors can be expensive. There are different types of actions and the processes to deal with them are different. Remember too that within a corporate action type each may be slightly different.

Key to the process of corporate actions is credible data and meeting deadlines. The latter involves not just dealer/fund manager/client in decision making and resulting instructions but also the CSDs and custodians.

Controls must reflect the three stages:

1 Capturing corporate action details
2 Decision
3 Instruction

Reconciliations

Characteristics:

> **A process, that can be manual or automated, and provides evidence of the agreement of various positions, actions and instructions.**

Key elements of the process

- Timing
- Positions
  - Intra-day
  - End of Day
  - Trade day + 1
- Settlement values
  - Consideration
  - Initial margin
  - Variation margin
  - Option premium
- Confirms of trades to deal tickets
- Cash position/ledger balance
- Assets
  - Held (physical and in custody)
  - Loaned
  - Pending settlement
  - Used as collateral
- Value-dated payments and receipts
- Nostro/bank reconciliations
- Profit/loss account
- Collateral

A high-profile and critical process is reliant on the skills of the reconciling team and the source and quality of the data to be reconciled. A failure in reconciliation of positions, profit/loss, exposures, payments, etc. can, and usually does, result in financial loss. Sometimes it can be so serious that the very business is threatened.

Automated reconciliation enables exceptions to be identified quickly and resolved. However, some reconciliation is still on a manual check basis and there must be special controls to ensure completeness and timing of these reconciliations.

Exception and resolution reports from reconcilations teams are a vital part of the overall, operations risk management function.

Key controls need to cover:

- Timing
- Method, i.e. automated (quality and security of systems) or manual (experience of personnel)
- Management of exceptions and over-ageing

Client settlement

Characteristic:

Process of supplying settlement data to the client and taking action to effect the movement or holding of cash, assets, collateral, etc. in settlement of the transactions as per procedures and instructions agreed with the client.

Key elements of the process

- Production of settlement information
- Automatic/overnight-associated reconciliation timing
- Instruction confirmation and processing

- Trigger payment instructions
- Collateral management
- Custodian/agent Instructions
- Daily and periodic valuations and reporting

The processes associated with client settlement and the added-value services that might be offered are core activities. The generation of the records of the client's transactions, positions, ledger balances, etc. are fundamentals of client service. Added to this we can look at collateral, centralized clearing and various custody services that are provided daily or periodically.

Controls over the accuracy of the data including reconciliation are paramount, so too are controls over basic processes like instructions. Here the controls are needed over the authorization of instructions, changes to any standard settlement instructions (SSIs), etc. Operations must carry out due diligence in ensuring that what they are doing and being asked to do are in the client's interests and/or conform to the agreed procedures. In some cases there are strict regulatory requirements surrounding client settlement, for example segregation of client assets from those of the firm and the prohibition on using one client's money to cover another client's shortfall.

Proper controls to ensure that all client trades are accounted for, that all payments have been made or received and that any additional instructions related to say collateral, corporate actions, etc. are essential.

Asset management, funding and cash management

Characteristic:

> **A largely automated function that places and borrows funds to facilitate settlement and client added-value services including foreign exchange transactions.**

Key elements of the process

- Deadlines
- Allocation of collateral for margin calls
- Source of funding for cash settlement
- Payment instructions and conditions (delivery versus payment, payment versus payment, free of payment)
- Payments/receipts of currencies
- Securities borrowing/lending
- Repos

A multi-process task that has as its objective the efficient settlement of securities and derivatives, as well as the management of benefits, cash flows and assets, controls over the cash and asset management are critical in terms of risk management.

Fraud is a key issue here and controls need to be robust and effective in detecting unusual instructions, values, amounts or destinations that perhaps indicate fraudulent activity.

Primary controls are related to the segregation of duties internally that will prevent personnel with access to trading, trade input, positions or account data management from being able to make or instruct payments.

Similarly there needs to be segregation of duties for those responsible for the movement of assets whether in relation to settlement or for collateral and stock lending/borrowing purposes. Specific controls over bearer securities are needed as the potential for theft or misuse is high given their characteristics.

Issues such as money laundering are also important and managers must ensure compliance with the money-laundering rules in the locations in which the firm and its clients undertake business. Controls to prevent and/or then to deal with a suspected money-laundering situation must be in place and regularly reviewed and updated. Unfortunately some products such as derivatives lend themselves to the purpose of money laundering and it is essential that the operations team are alert to this fact. Basic characteristics of many exchange-traded derivatives (and some OTCs) such as delivery, initial and variation margin produce daily and periodic movements of both assets and, more importantly, cash. Thus a money launderer could seek to open a large position in futures, cover the initial margin with 'dirty' money, close the position a few days later and take back 'clean' money.

Equally the launderer may ask the organization to purchase, say, Treasury bills to utilize as collateral or bonds to be used in the delivery process for the bond future. In both cases dirty money is converted to clean money or assets.

Particularly important is to note and report any changes to payment instructions as this may well be perfectly acceptable but equally could be an attempt to route clean money to the launderer's accounts.

Management information

Characteristic:

> **The preparation of data mostly automated but sometimes manually of data needed for the purposes of monitoring and measuring performance, risk management and routine controls.**

Key elements of the process

- Production of data on settlement fails, delays and resultant claims
- Production of funding exposure – predicted, actual and intra-day
- Record of reconciliation breaks and time to resolution

- Evidence of reasonableness of profit/loss data versus actual settlement
- requirements
- Justification of 'large' payments, settlement instruction changes, etc.
- List of breaches of controls
- Production of costs analysis
- Performance analysis

Management information is often drawn from the same data source as the day-to-day processes. It is collated and then compared against benchmarks and other data sources. Controls are needed to establish a credible source of management information. They are also needed, given the confidentiality and sensitivity of the data, over the distribution of the information. In most organizations there are two types of management information: general information for distribution to team leaders etc. and confidential information for distribution to senior personnel.

To many Operations staff the generation of management information can be viewed as time-consuming and irrelevant. To some there is also a suspicion that it may be used for purposes related to them such as their own performance. As a result there may be an indifference shown to any errors or missing data that is incorporated into management information. Controls to prevent such an occurrence are essential as any corrupt data in decision making or risk management can be disastrous

Developing controls

Having identified the core processes and recognized the areas in need of controls the next stage is to create the right type of controls. This is very important. The controls must be effective but workable. If the control is too onerous it will take too much time and resource to be practical. On the other hand, if it is inadequate it will leave the business open to unacceptable levels of risk. In the preceding pages we have mentioned fundamental controls such as segregation of duties, authorization, etc. What other controls are workable and where can they be used?

Procedures are a crucial part of the Operations function and also form part of the control function. The procedures manual is therefore an integral part of the control process and provides details of what action staff should take in given scenarios. The downside is that many either reject the procedure manual as an effective tool because it is usually too bulky and unstructured to be of any use while others confuse the procedures manual and an operations manual. An operations manual is likely to be about detailed processes associated with, say, systems. The procedures manual, on the other hand, should show the train of events and relevant actions for those events in a given process. We look at procedures and procedure documentation in Chapter 7.

Sign-off is another type of control that requires one, two or more signatures as evidence that an action should take place. The signatures will be those of experienced senior staff and managers in various combinations for varying degrees of perceived importance of the action. For example, a payment of several million dollars may need the authority of two senior managers.

Tolerances are useful controls designed to prevent the input of data outside certain parameters. A simple example would be a price of an instrument or an interest rate where someone could inadvertently enter, say, 61p instead of 16p or 61% instead of 6.1%. By requiring the person inputting the data to confirm the value of the field there is a chance to avoid an error.

Flagging of critical times or situations can also act as an effective control. For instance, both corporate actions and derivative settlement teams rely on event diaries to inform them of when a situation will occur or is likely to occur. It is a simple enough process although it does rely on the quality of the data and so the database management team becomes a significant control feature but also a risk source.

Bearing in mind that controls may need to take into account not only internal considerations but also external ones such as regulations, timing for instructions to custodians and sub-custodians as well as clearing houses, we need to be aware of deadlines, conventions time-zones, holidays and communication methods in designing controls.

Obviously a control that only picks up and flags the fact that a call on a rights issue is due today at one minute past midnight UK time is of little use if the rights issue is on an Australian stock where it is already half-way through the following morning. By the time someone in the UK office sees the flag it will be mid to late afternoon and far too late to do anything about taking up the rights. Action, and therefore the control was needed at least 24 hours earlier. You may consider this to be an extreme example, but it would only be avoided if there were other controls that ensured a corporate action on an overseas security was flagged and action taken in good time.

This is why controls must be workable and not just there because they would prevent a problem. To avoid an error on trade input you could have a control that checks the input. But what if the control failed? You could have another control that checked the control that checked the input. But what happens if that control failed? How many controls do you put in place? Controls need to be reasonable, based on the potential risk impact of a problem and the likelihood of occurrence.

Controls can be very much system based as well as being by oversight, i.e. a manager reviewing data. They have two objectives, one to prevent an error and the other to deter deliberate abuse or criminal acts. If a control or series of controls is seen to be unworkable and therefore are frequently ignored or circumvented then a significant weakness has been created. The same will occur if the control highlights any problem however small or irrelevant. The control will lack credibility and if and when it does identify the big problem the chances are that it will not work because people are not paying any attention to the data.

Controls are crucially important and operations managers need to take time to analyse the type of control that is truly suited to a process. Then they need to decide how the control should be monitored and managed and finally they need to know how effective the control is. Once we have identified processes and the controls for the processes we are ready to map the risk.

Chapter 6

Mapping risk

Mapping operations risk involves identifying what the source of the risk is, what its impact might be and what controls there are to mitigate the risk. One very early question we need to ask is, what level of risk are we talking about? If we want to map every risk however small across the whole Operations function then clearly we are talking about a very major undertaking for most organizations. We do, of course, want to have a meaningful mapping of risk but it is my view that the mapping should be relevant and only include risks that have one or more of the following characteristics:

- Likely to be systemic
- Can result in a single financial loss greater than *X* where *X* is determined by the size of the organization and the loss figure it would deem significant to its business
- Can result in a multiple or repetitive loss situation that would be greater than *X* where *X* is determined by the size of the organization and the loss figure it would deem significant to the business
- Could result individually or systemically or by repetition in some sort of direct or indirect regulatory risk situation
- Would be likely to cause visible or invisible loss of reputation
- Is a risk that if it occurs will be detrimental to the performance of the Operations function

There are other criteria that could be included and it is very important that the mapping process is right and relevant to the organization.

Once the mapping parameters are decided the process, or rather the processes of mapping, can start. First, we need to undertake a full workflow analysis of all the core and secondary processes so that we have a complete picture of what the operation function actually does. Some of these processes will be daily and continuous, some will be daily but intermittent and others will be periodic but at set times or periodic and at variable times. Within the workflow analysis we will need the expected duration of tasks, average resource levels etc. plus the extent to which the process is automated or manual. A relatively simple analysis can be constructed by tracking the flow of a process, and then all the processes through a day. See Figure 6.1.

The workflow analysis can be as detailed or general as is required. Figure 6.1 is a fairly general analysis and, for instance, the European markets could be split into individual markets, particularly if specific teams deal with those markets.

The objectives of the analysis are:

- To show the processes and their duration
- To show where there are concentrations of processes
- To show where there are similar processes taking place

This level of analysis is useful as it shows the expected duration of the working day related to specific functions. Comparison with management information on the actual duration of tasks will highlight performance issues and point towards possible risk scenarios forming.

However, a better picture of risk will be obtained by overlaying a second analysis onto the workflow. This looks at the resource levels available compared to the duration of the tasks or processes and begins to deliver answers to further objectives which are:

- To identify potential weaknesses in the operations function
- To manage resource levels

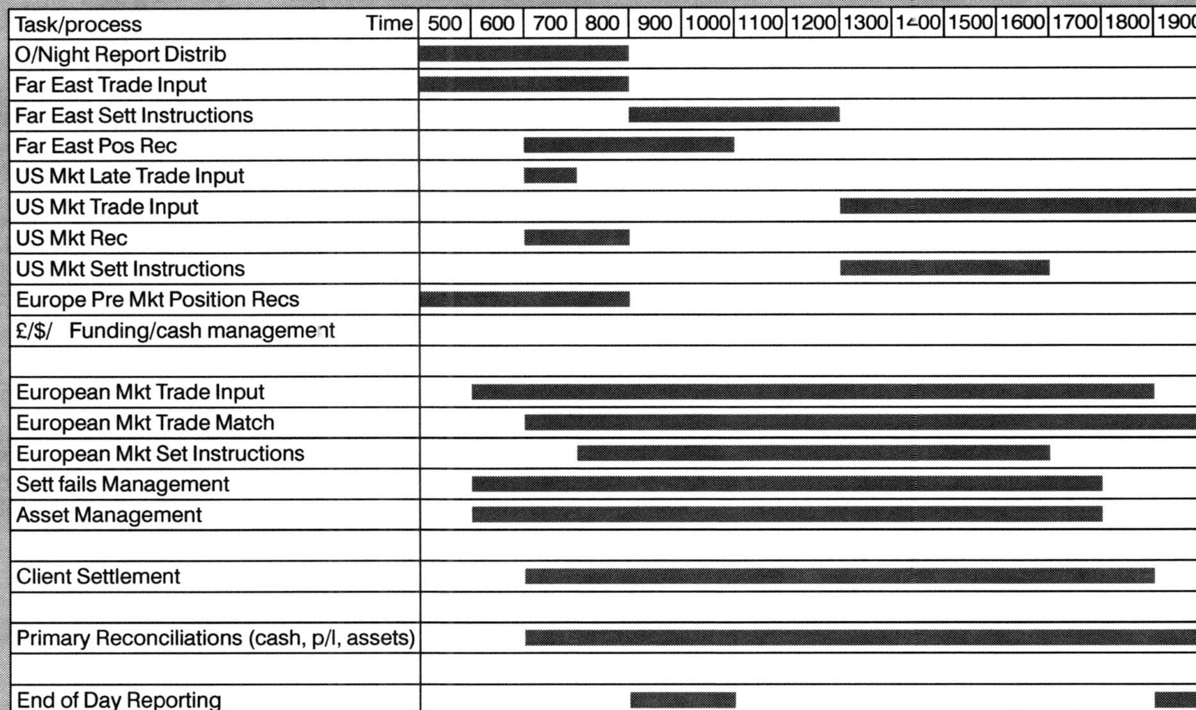

Figure 6.1 A workflow analysis template. (*Source*: Computer Based Learning Ltd)

- To identify areas where there is significant gain to be had from a change to procedures and processes, including automation

Illustrating the level of activity associated with a process at a given time can further enhance the analysis. So we show the expected peaks and troughs in volume, deadlines, etc. and this enables us to see even more clearly where a weakness and therefore a risk may exist. The workflow analysis has provided a twofold benefit.

We now understand the work that is being done by the department and we can see potential problem areas that also indicate a potential risk. Although the initial analysis process may take time and possibly a few attempts to get it as we want, once completed it can and must be continuously reviewed and updated, and this is a far easier task.

At this point it is worth noting that the management of workflow is in itself a control process and a valuable aid to the Operations manager. Workflow analysis is desirable anyway whether or not it is also used to help identify and track risk.

Risk mapping

The policy towards mapping risk will vary from one organization to another. Fund management companies will have different processes and workflow to an international multi-location investment bank with a large principal and client activity in a wide variety of products. It does no harm at all to look at the different ways organizations approach the subject of risk. Very often the best operations and operational risk management policies and procedures that I have seen involve a variety of methods and strategies taken from several sources and in a few cases active cooperation on risk management by organizations.

Mapping operations risk can be done in a similar way to workflow analysis. By tracking the risk not only through the operations area but

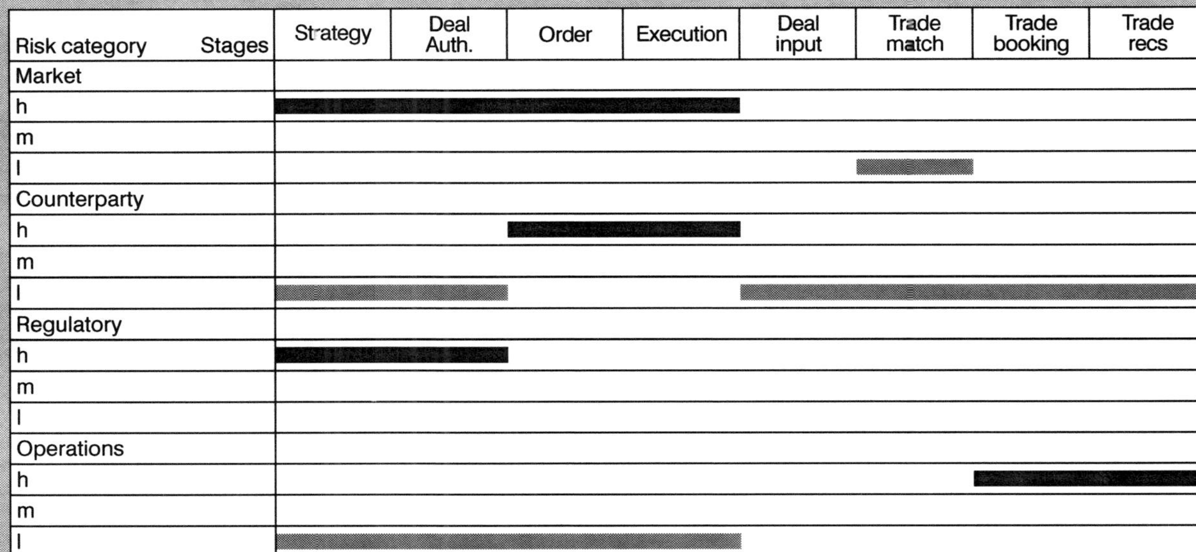

Figure 6.2 Risk tracking and procedures plan for an exchange-traded call option

also other areas the extent of systemic risk can be determined. Figure 6.2 shows how the risk moves from high to low within an area as the process moves forward.

What the two analysis processes have given us is a view of where risk is and how it moves around within the organization. We can now look at different ways to interpret the data. One method of doing this is to use ‘envelopes’, ‘volcanoes’ and ‘waves’, all of which help to measure the risk and its impact. There are many other ways in which risk can be identified, mapped and analysed. The main issue once this process is complete is to understand the probability of the risk manifesting itself into a problem. To fully complete the picture we need to look at measuring the impact of the risk.

Chapter 7

Measuring risk and the effect of controls

How do you measure operations or, for that matter, operational risk? Consider again the ideas of the BIS on measuring operational risk.

II. Risk Management: Identification, Measurement, Monitoring and Control Principle 4: Banks should identify the operational risk inherent in all types of products, activities, processes and systems. Banks should also ensure that before new products, activities, processes and systems are introduced or undertaken the operational risk inherent in them is subject to adequate assessment procedures.

25. *Risk identification is critical for the subsequent development of viable operational risk measurement, monitoring and control. Effective risk identification considers both internal factors (such as the complexity of the bank's structure, the nature of the banks activities, the quality of personnel, organisational changes and employee turnover) and external factors (such as fluctuating economic conditions, changes in the industry and technological advances) that could adversely affect the achievement of the bank's objectives.*

26. *The risk identification process should also include a determination of which risks are controllable by the bank to help them identify operational risk:*
    - *Self- or Risk-Assessment: a bank assesses its operations and activities against a menu of operational risk events. This process is internally driven and often incorporates checklists and/or workshops to identify the strengths and weaknesses of the operational risk environment.*
    - *Risk Mapping: in this process, various business units, organisation functions or process flows are mapped by risk type. This exercise can reveal areas of weakness and help prioritise subsequent management action.*
    - *Key Risk Indicators: risk indicators are statistics and/or metrics, often financial which can provide insight into a bank's risk position. These indicators should be reviewed on a periodic basis (often monthly or quarterly) to alert banks to changes that may be indicative of risk concerns. Such indicators may include for example the number of failed trades, staff turnover rates and the frequency and/or severity of errors and omissions.*
    - *Threshold/limits: typically tied to risk indicators, threshold levels (or changes) in key risk indicators, when exceeded, alert management to areas of potential problems.*
    - *Scorecards: these provide a means of translating a qualitative assessments into quantitative metrics that can be used to allocate economic capital to business lines in relation to performance in managing and controlling various aspects of operational risk.*

Principle 5: Banks should establish the processes necessary for measuring operational risk.

27. *Measuring operational risk requires both estimating the probability of an operational loss event and the potential size of the loss. All banks should engage in tracking group-wide operational risk*

data. Such information is fundamental to measuring, monitoring and controlling operational risk exposure. For any reliable measurement system, data would need to be collected in order to develop general measures of operational risk. While the nature of the data collected may vary across banks, to be useful, the breadth, history and integrity of the data collected must be commensurate with the bank's operational risk profile and approach to managing risk.

28 Under this principle, banks should develop sound internal reporting practices and systems that are consistent with the scope of operational risk defined by supervisors and the banking industry. In addition, banks should have an operational risk measurement methodology, knowledgeable staff and an appropriate systems infrastructure capable of identifying and gathering operational risk data.

Source: Basel Committee on Banking Supervision December 2001 Bank for International Settlements

Is this really a totally appropriate way to measure and quantify the risk or should we consider also the subjective way of looking at risk, particularly operations risk? We can study combining measuring methods with the subjective views of those who really know the extent of the risk, the operations managers.

The Australian Financial Markets Association (AFMA) developed a process for managing operational risk called SCOR (Standards for the Control of Operational Risk Management). SCOR was developed jointly by members of the Australian Financial Operations Association (AFOA) and the AFMA and project managed by Arthur Andersen. It was launched in November 1999 as a 'Best Practice' standard for treasury operations and OTC financial markets. The reasons AFMA give for the development and my observations on SCOR are as follows.

During the 1990s, a now-infamous incident destroyed one international merchant bank in a blaze of publicity. That bank was Barings and it suffered as much from fraud perpetrated by a senior trader as it did from operational risk management failure. Barings, among other things, failed to separate its front- and back-office functions. This is a basic tenet of operational risk management. Recently, an Australian company suffered an operational risk management failure, which cost it A$45 million, plus legal costs. This case went to the courts.

The AFMA poses some interesting questions. Could your company afford a similar fate? Do you recognize and manage operational risks in your company? Does your board and senior management know that there is an industry standard? Is your company compliant?

SCOR is a blueprint for identifying and managing operational risk. It defines operational risk as the risk that an institution will suffer substantial reputation damage or financial loss as a result of a breakdown in human resources, processes or technology. This may occur as a result of inadequate operational policies or procedures, including systems, infrastructure and controls, human error or management failure, fraudulent, malicious or intentional acts, both internal and external, and uncontrollable or unmanageable events. Risk factors include fraud, illegal acts and compliance issues. But leadership, staff training, infrastructure, integrity, product development and the operating environment are also operational risk factors.

A company that fails to keep adequate records to support trading activities is at risk of operational failure. Also a company that fails to ensure staff take a minimum of two weeks' consecutive leave each year may also be at risk. The SCOR document states that staff rotation, or relieving a trader in a senior position for a minimum of two weeks each year, is highly likely to lead to the exposure of trading anomalies, if any exist. Exactly the same situation applies to operations managers and supervisors.

Designed to help treasury managers manage risk, SCOR covers five Australian OTC markets: foreign exchange, cash and discount securities, fixed interest and repurchase agreements. But it provides a solid framework for the discovery and management of operational risk for corporations from any sector and of any size. SCOR can be used by any organization as a benchmarking tool because it sets common protocols and establishes the use of a common language to identify and manage operational risk. SCOR identifies more than a hundred operational risk management factors, and delivers a minimum or recommended standard to market participants. It identifies risks and tells you why it is necessary to recognize and manage that risk.

SCOR enables senior management and boards to measure effective operational risk management compliance. It is designed to deliver:

- Reduced exposure to risk
- Best practice standards
- Reduced error rates
- A set of common standards
- Improved efficiencies
- Reduced audit costs

Again the AFMA in their marketing blurb ask crucial operational risk questions. Do you know if your trading staff take at least two weeks, consecutive leave each year? Do you know that if your company suffered a systems failure whether it could survive? Do you know if you have the right documentation in place to monitor new products?

This is good in terms of the actual management of risk and I would encourage the reader to go to AFMA's website (see the Appendix) and download the full details. Many of the standards in SCOR can be applied and/or adapted to most types of business and organizations in the financial markets.

But equally within the Operations teams we need to be able to illustrate why measuring and controlling risk is so important. The importance of measuring the risk impact can be illustrated by the 'risk volcano' (Figure 7.1).

Figure 7.1 The risk volcano

What is the risk volcano? As we know, a volcano can be subject to a very violent explosion of pressure or it can be a serene, inactive and not unattractive mountain. We can draw parallels with the operations function or the operational risk environment in a business. With a volcano there is often very little to indicate that anything is happening deep down inside the earth and, to all intents and purposes, the volcano is extinct. So sure of this are some people that they build homes within the vicinity or even on the volcano itself. Are they being complacent or just taking a calculated gamble on the risk? The same applies to an operations function. It could appear on the face of it that there seems to be no problems and no reason to be unduly worried. But, just like a volcano, it may not be all that it seems.

In Figure 7.2 the outward appearance is calm and uninteresting and yet inside there is activity (the shaded area). This activity may be powerful but it is contained by the structure.

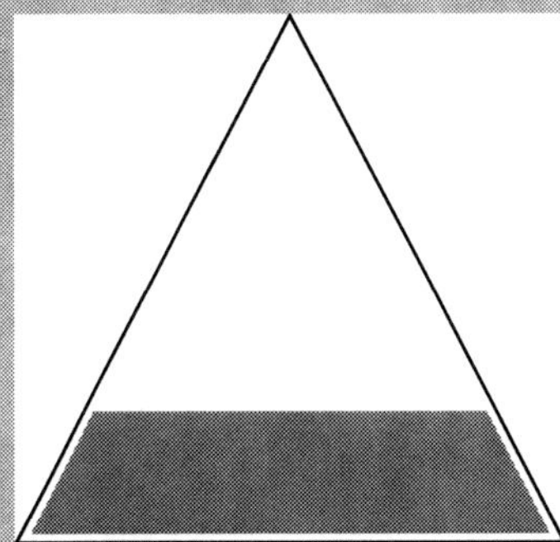

Figure 7.2 The risk volcano: apparently quiescent

In Figure 7.3 we see that the activity level has increased and now there are some telltale signs that all is no longer serene and inactive. Smoke appears from the top and maybe some evidence of the pressure building up appears on the structure. We know that the chance of the volcano erupting is increasing and unless the pressure is reduced the volcano will blow.

Instead of the example of the volcano, use the operations function. Problems are increasing and the occasional telltale sign is emerging,

Figure 7.3 The risk volcano: pressure builds up

maybe an increase in errors or settlement fails. If this is not addressed the pressure will continue to build and the end result will ultimately be like that of the volcano, an uncontrollable eruption of errors, problems and issues that may be devastating in their impact.

We can look at Barings to see just how this volcano scenario can happen. Everything looked fine but then signs that things were not quite right started to appear. The exchange asked questions, so did others, the funding levels were becoming very significant. Nothing was done and in the end the pressure was too much and as the unidentified and uncontrolled situation continued the money ran out with devastating consequences for the bank.

So we can use the risk volcano to show how a failure to recognize that risk is always there and then failure to see the pressure on the risk increasing can ultimately create an uncontrollable risk situation.

So how can we measure the likelihood of risk occurring and what the impact will be? One way is to use 'risk envelopes' and 'risk waves'.

Risk envelopes

Risk envelopes are a simple method of identifying where risk starts and how it progresses. We can establish our risk envelopes as shown in Table 7.1.

Table 7.1 Operational risk envelopes

Trade capture	Reputation
Money laundering & fraud	Custody
Cash management	Personnel
Market risks	Reconciliations
Systems and STP	Reporting
Regulation and compliance	Settlement

When we identify a risk we allocate it to each of the envelopes that it has an impact on to help us understand where the risk is occurring. For example, we might consider a settlement fail. Where does the risk occur? The answer could be:

- Market risks – we may be unable to settle another trade because of the fail
- Reputation – if we now fail or cause the fail our reputation is damaged
- Regulatory – if we are the cause we may be in breach of clearing house rules
- Settlement – our asset positions are incorrect and we may need to borrow
- Cash management – our funding requirement may change because of the fail(s) and as a result we may lose interest and incur overdraft charges

The risk is not contained and the risk may be greater in certain envelopes than others.

To help us analyse this we can again use relatively simple data as shown in Figure 7.4.

This analysis is showing us the risk scenario, the projected occurrence rate and severity of the risk on a scale of 1 to 10 plus any existing controls that mitigate the risk. In addition it shows the other risk areas where it might impact. The combination of envelopes and risk/controls analysis is giving us an almost complete picture of the risk environment. However, there are still issues to be considered.

First, is risk constant and second, how do we obtain the above analysis? The simple answer to the first question is, no it is not constant and the overall risk for an operations department will be complex and variable. We will use 'risk waves' to incorporate this factor into the risk analysis process.

Source/Risk Heading	Occurrence /Severity	Settlement	System	Counterparty	Personnel	Regulatory	Legal	Reputation	Market	Financial
Risk Scenario										
Example										
Interest rate incorrect		Yes	Yes	Yes				Yes		Yes
Occurrence	*6*									
Severity	*8*									
Control	*-17*									
Total	***-3***									
Scale	10 high	1 low								
Occ/Sev = +/10										
Control = minus/20										

Figure 7.4 Risk analysis mapping template

The 'risk wave' is an analysis that sees the risk and then tries to plot that risk in terms of the normal or acceptable level of risk. If we take the risk/control analysis in Figure 7.4, the risk value is −3, indicating that the controls are more than adequate to manage the risk, currently. But what if that figure were to change to +3? What has caused this change? Maybe the process or procedures have been changed so that either the risk occurrence or severity, or both, is greater. Perhaps the controls have been changed with a resultant fall in their effectiveness. Whatever it is, it will affect the overall level of risk level of the Operations function and the reason must be identified, with suitable remedial action agreed and implemented by the managers. Figure 7.5 explains the theory behind this measurement technique.

In the figure we can look at wave A. This is a risk or combination of risks and situations that has raised the normal level of the operations risk. In fact it has raised it above a reportable threshold where the Operations manager would need to make the group risk manager or management team aware of the situation. The risk management team would now decide on any actions that might be prudent, including

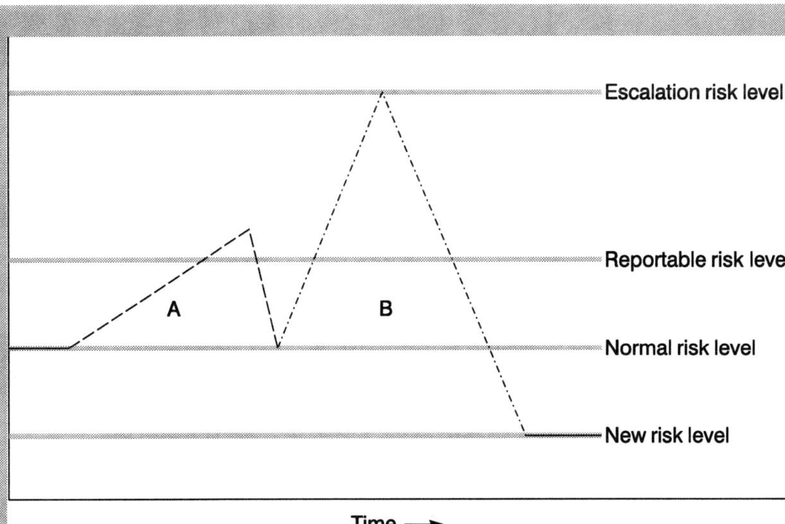

Figure 7.5 An example of a risk wave. (*Source*: Computer Based Learning Ltd)

setting aside additional capital. However, at this stage it is more of a warning than a 'needs action' situation and provided the manager can explain the reasons and the expected duration of the wave little else needs to be done than to monitor it. Such a situation might be a new product where there is a period of increased risk while controls and procedures are introduced and, once successful, the risk returns to the normal or expected level.

Wave B would be a more significant situation with a steeper risk wave. This almost reaches escalation level, which would mean that the Operations manager was no longer in sole control and the risk group would be looking at various contingencies. Such a situation might be the introduction of a new system. Here the risk rises massively as the system beds in and then ultimately falls again to such an extent that the normal risk level is actually reduced as the benefits of the new system and automation reduce the risk.

Figure 7.5 shows the waves and expected duration. The actual duration would be plotted over this to enable monitoring and control.

As far as the second question is concerned, the analysis is rather subjective and when used is usually based on the perceptions of the managers and supervisors. There is nothing at all wrong with this because, as I have said, they are by far the best people to perform the analysis. What we do need to do is recognize that the views of managers and supervisors may be affected such that they over- or understate the analysis. To overcome this we can utilize the available management to try to confirm the validity or otherwise of the analysis or, alternatively, have an independent assessment made, either using other managers, audit input and/or external consultants.

The process is not perfect, but then it is not designed to show the risk to the last pennies or cents. It is not market or credit risk we are analysing but operations and operational environments where risk is about errors and resource rather than exposure.

We have seen how risk can be identified, measured and controlled through various relatively simple analysis processes. The most crucial thing with the measuring of operations and operational risk is to find a happy level between modelling and subjective observation.

Any business should set aside capital against possible risk, and operational risk is no exception. As part of operational risk, operations risk therefore will consume some element of capital. The extent of that capital requirement depends very much on the efficiency of the operations teams in their day-to-day work and also on the ability of the manager to take the process a stage further and control the possible risks to the point where they are no longer relevant. Once achieved, however, there must now be a continuous process of monitoring, measuring and analysing.

Risk can impact slowly and be devastating in its impact. Equally it can be swift and just as devastating. Like the sea, it can change from friend to bitter enemy in minutes. It is therefore important to respect risk but at the same time not be overawed by it. After all, risk in operations and operational environments is largely controlled by effective procedures and by the skills of people.

Chapter 8

Procedures

The Operations function is all about procedures, more procedures and then even more procedures. Procedures are there for systems, for settlement, for payments and for dealing with instructions. Just about everything else that happens in a day for an Operations team is governed by procedures. They are at the heart of the Operations functions and are therefore critically important if the function is to be successful.

There are procedures that enable a specific process to occur and procedures that link processes. The skill with procedures is to design them carefully, review then constantly and update them as frequently as is needed. Most inefficient organizations have outdated procedures for dealing with the business they undertake.

The proper documenting of procedures is also important and this can be illustrated through a typical process of an activity within, for example, a treasury department, first, in text format at keystroke level followed by the same activity illustrated as a flow diagram. Let us look at an example.

Example

DIVISION: TRADE SETTLEMENTS
Department: Cash Management
Procedure: 30–07 Telegraphic Transfers (XYZ Bank CHAPS)

Introduction

This document describes the procedure to input telegraphic transfer payments into the XYZ CHAPS terminal. The procedure has three stages: input, authorization and transmission. Payments cannot be input and authorized by the same operator. Payments are made in settlement of trades or cash transfers at the request of clients.

Care must be taken with all payments as there is the **risk** of the firm losing money through interest claims and its reputation being damaged by upsetting the client.

The XYZ CHAPS terminal is located in the secure communications room. The procedure must be completed by **14:45** each day.

Table 8.1 Contents

Receiving telegraphic transfer instructions

Telegraphic transfers are prepared by and received from the Cash Transfer Department throughout the day.

Refer to the Cash Transfer Department procedure:
30–06 Preparation of Telegraphic Transfers.

Accessing the chaps terminal

To input the telegraphic transfer instructions ('the payments') into the XYZ CHAPS terminal, follow the steps below:

Place your XYZ security card into the reader. (Blue arrow facing up and forwards.)
Type in your **PIN**.
Press: **ENTER**.
Click on the **XYZ CHAPS** icon.
Type in your **Operator ID** and **password**.
Press: **ENTER**.

Testing the communications line

It is not possible to input a telegraphic transfer into the XYZ system until a communications link has been established. Test the availability of the communications line to the bank by following the steps below:

Click on **Global** menu item.
Click on **Communications** menu item.
Click on **Link Availability** menu item.
Click on **Send** menu item.
The system responds with a message *Line to Bank Available* or *Line to Bank Unavailable*.
If the line is unavailable, telephone XYZ CHAPS support desk (0900–123456) and report the difficulty.
Wait 15 minutes and check the line again.

Inputting payment instructions

The payment instructions include details of the beneficiary's bank and account number. To avoid non-receipt of funds, it is most important that payment details are input accurately. To input the payments, follow the steps below:

Click on **Payments** menu item.

Click on **Input Payments** menu item.

For each telegraphic transfer, enter the following details (using the **TAB** key to progress to the next field):

Amount: The amount to be transferred.

Account Number: The account number to be debited. Ensure that the correct account number is selected in accordance with the telegraphic transfer form.

If a beneficiary reference is shown on the telegraphic transfer form, enter it in the **Beneficiary** field. All remaining fields on the input screen will update automatically. Continue at **Saving the Input**.

If no beneficiary reference is shown on the telegraphic transfer form, enter the details below:

Beneficiary: The beneficiary sort-code.

Account Number: The beneficiary account number at the recipient bank.

Beneficiary Name: The account name at the recipient bank.

Address: Leave blank.

Bank Name: The name of the recipient bank.

Address: Enter the town or city in which the recipient bank is located.

Ordering Customer: Universal Stockbrokers.

Ordering Institution: Universal Stockbrokers.

Payment Details: Universal Stockbrokers.

On the next line, enter any further reference appearing in the **Ref** field of the telegraphic transfer form.

Saving the input

The authorizer cannot access unsaved payments. To save the payments, follow the steps below:

Click on the **Save** button.
When all telegraphic transfers have been processed, click on the **Cancel** button to close the session.
Remove your security card from the reader.
Request the duty authorizer to **authorize** the payments.
Place the telegraphic transfer forms in the **pending** tray adjacent to the CHAPS terminal.

Authorizing payments

The telegraphic transfer payments are authorized via the XYZ CHAPS terminal. *Payments cannot be input and authorized by the same person.* To avoid non-receipt of funds, it is most important that payment details are checked accurately. To authorize the payments, follow the steps below:

Place your XYZ security card into the reader. (Blue arrow facing up and forwards.)
Type in your **PIN** and press **Enter**.
Click on the **XYZ CHAPS** icon.
Type in your **Operator ID** and **password**.
Press **ENTER**.
Click on the **payments** menu item.
Click on the **authorize** menu item.
Highlight all outstanding payments by clicking on the first item and dragging the pointer to the last item then click on the **Select** button.
The first payment will automatically appear on the screen.
Check **carefully** all displayed details against the telegraphic transfer form.
If the details are correct, click on the **Authorize** button and sign the **Verified** box on the telegraphic transfer form.

If any detail is incorrect note the incorrect payment and click on the **Next** button. *Do not click on the Authorize button.*

If an incorrect payment is accidentally authorized, immediately inform the transmitter that the payment must not be transmitted.

When all items have been processed, click on the **Cancel** button to close the session.

Remove your security card from the reader.

Put the telegraphic transfer forms in the **pending** tray adjacent to the CHAPS terminal.

Inform the inputter that items have been authorized.

Provide the inputter with details of incorrect items that have not been authorized.

Correcting errors

The inputter must correct any input errors identified by the authorizer, as follows:

Type in your **Operator ID** and **password**.

Press **Enter**.

Select the **View Payments** option.

Press **Enter**.

Highlight the erroneous item and click on the **Amend** button.

Enter the correct details and click on the **Save** button.

Click on the **Cancel** button when all items have been corrected.

Request the duty authorizer to **authorize** the payments. See the section **Authorizing Payments**.

When all items have been successfully input and authorized, the inputter informs a staff member authorized to transmit payments (the transmitter) that there are items ready for transmission.

Transmitting payments

To transmit the payment instructions to the bank via the XYZ CHAPS terminal, follow the steps below:

Place your XYZ security card into the reader. (Blue arrow facing up and forwards.)

Type in your **PIN** and press **Enter**.

Click on the **XYZ CHAPS** icon.

Type in your **Operator ID** and **password**.

Press **Enter**.

Click on the **Payments** menu item.

Click on the **Transmit Payments** menu item.

Highlight all outstanding payments by clicking on the first item and dragging the pointer to the last item then click on the **Select** button.

The first payment will automatically appear on the screen.

Check all displayed details against the telegraphic transfer form.

If the details are correct, click on the **Transmit** button. A record of the payment will be printed.

If any detail is incorrect, note the incorrect payment and click on the **Next** button. *Do not click on the Transmit button.*

When all items have been processed, click on **Exit** to close the application.

Remove your security card from the reader.

Inform the inputter that items have been transmitted. Provide the inputter with details of erroneous items.

The original inputter must re-input the erroneous payments. (See section **Inputting payments**, above.)

The original authorizer must authorize the amended payments. (See section **Authorizing payments**, above.)

An authorized transmitter must transmit the corrected items. (See section **Transmitting Payments**, above.)

Stopping a payment

If an erroneous payment is accidentally transmitted, it must be stopped immediately by tested telex:

Telephone XYZ CHAPS support desk (0900–123456) and advise that a tested telex is being sent to stop a payment.

Complete a telex form giving the full details of the payment to be stopped.
Stamp the telex form with the **urgent** stamp.
Pass the telex form to the manager for **authorization**.
Take the authorized telex form to the telex room for **urgent testing** and transmission.
Telephone XYZ support desk to **confirm** that the message has been received and is being acted upon.

Filing telegraphic transfer forms

When all items have been successfully input, authorized and transmitted, the transmitter collects the completed telegraphic transfer forms from the secure room and passes them to the inputter for filing.
Completed telegraphic transfers are filed in the **cash book folder**.
Printouts of completed payments are filed in the **cash book folder**.
Procedure ends.

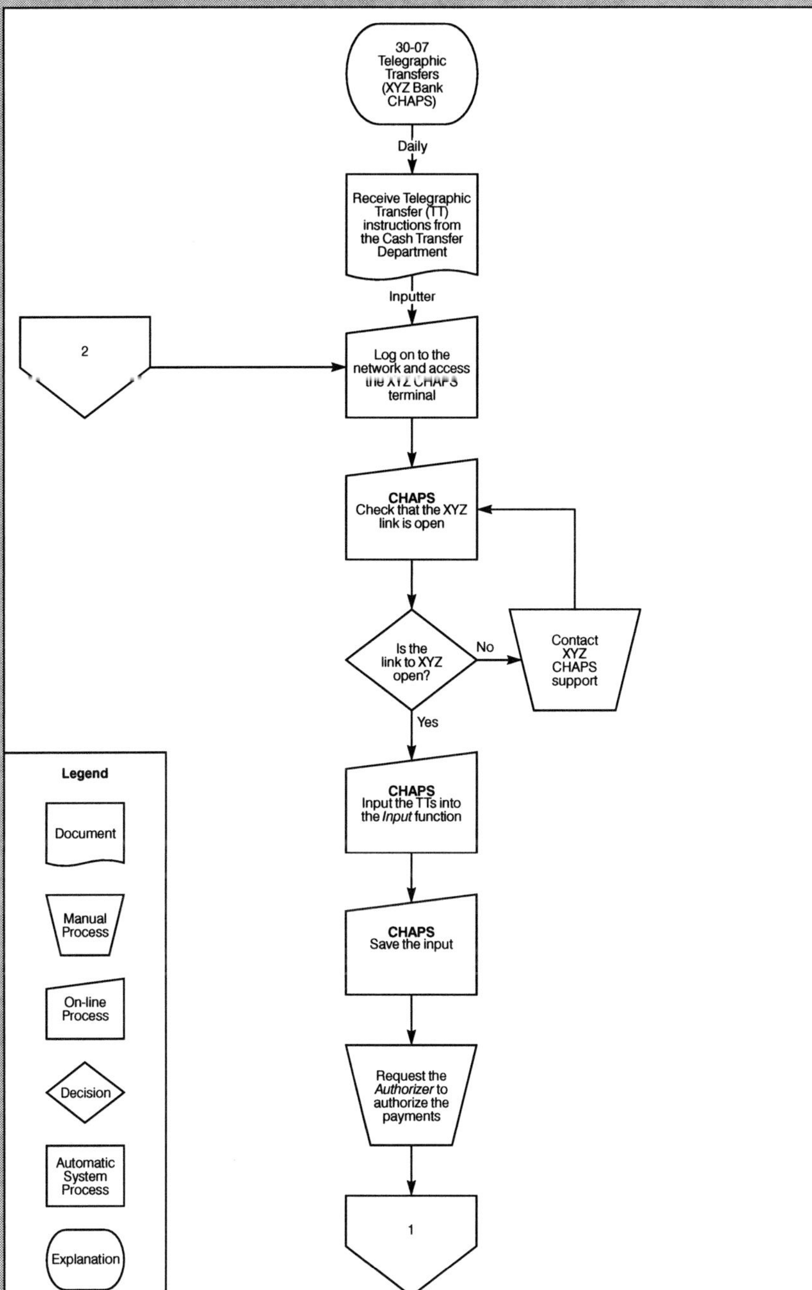

Figure 8.1 Example flow diagram: 1

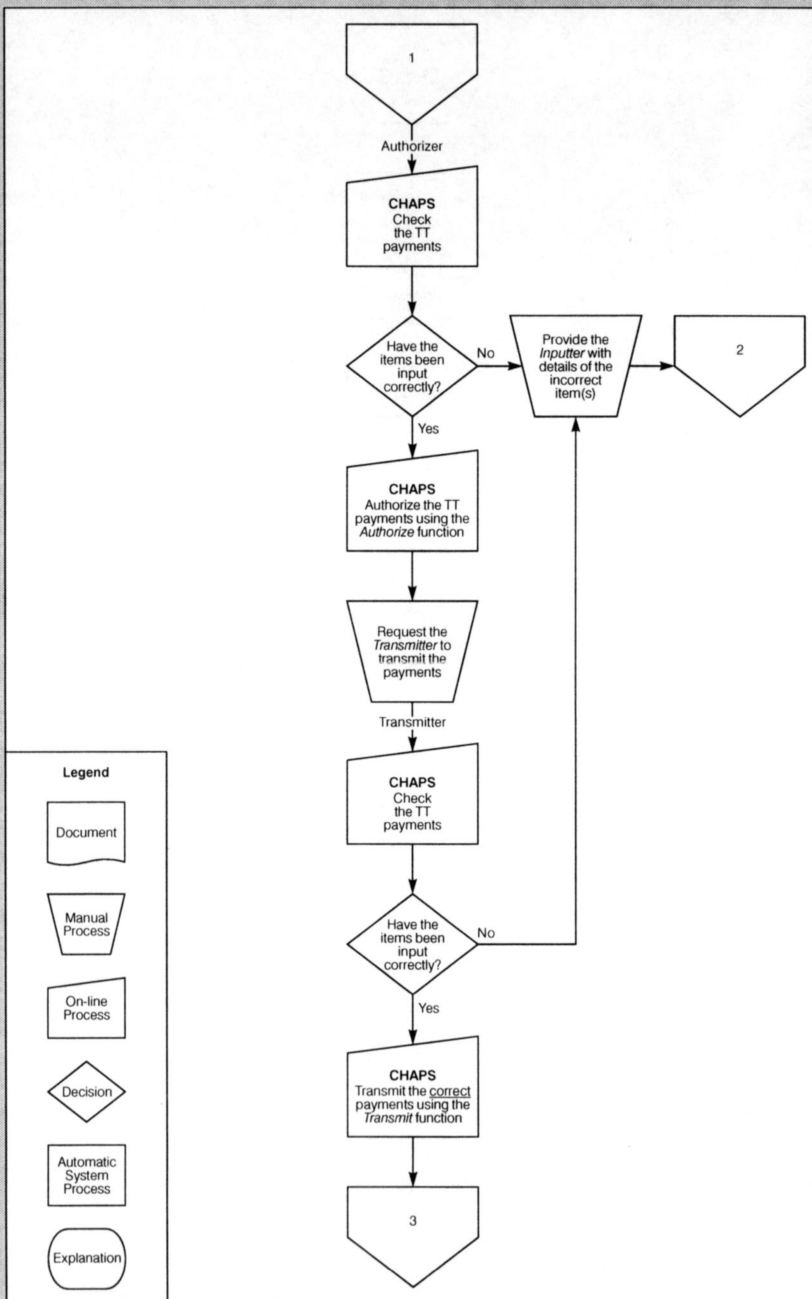

Figure 8.2 Example flow diagram: 2

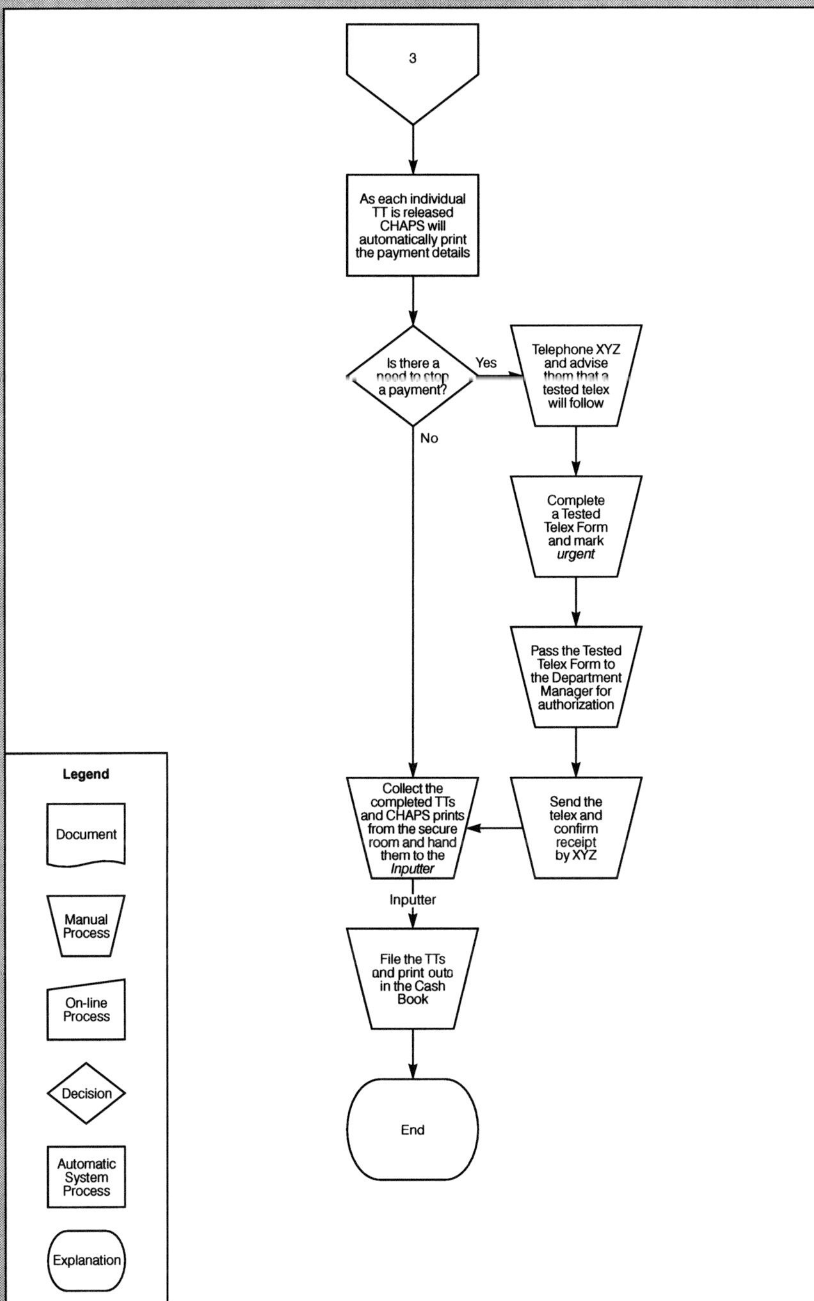

Figure 8.3 Example flow diagram: 3

The objectives of the procedures is to enable processes to be put in place that will become the working template for the function. Procedures fit into the overall process as shown in Figure 8.4. (The procedure flows in Figure 8.4 are reproduced by kind permission of The Procedure Documentation Company Ltd, a specialist organization dealing with reviewing and documenting procedures for all aspects of business. They are part of the DSC Portfolio and contact details can be found in Appendix 1.) Figure 8.4 gives the reader an idea of the way in which flows and procedures are designed and documented.

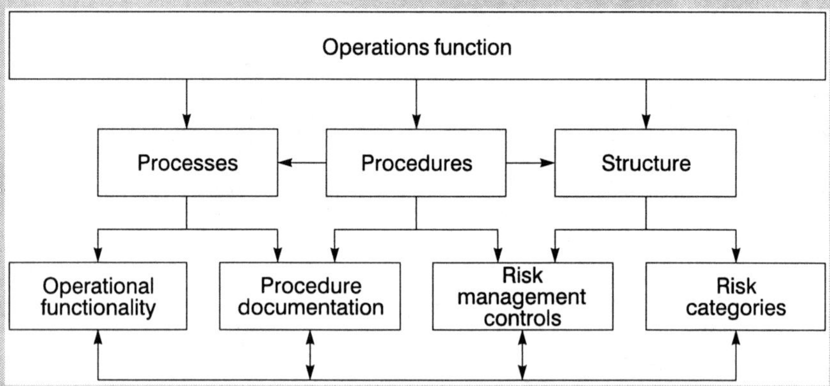

Figure 8.4 Procedure flows. (*Source*: The DSC Portfolio)

As noted earlier, the link between procedures and the structure of a department as well as the risk controls is at the heart of an Operations function. Poorly designed and out-of-date procedures will create problems and increase risk. Operations managers as part of the workflow analysis and risk mapping will see how effective procedures are and can make any necessary changes. Documented procedures enable personnel to see and understand how the processes work and interact. They also form an essential record for presentation to regulators and auditors to enable a benchmark of the performance of the Operations team to be made.

The regulatory issue is crucial as an inability to produce fully documented procedures for proposed business will result in refusal of a licence. Equally, evidence from an audit that shows that the procedures laid down are not being followed or are out of date may result in a suspension or withdrawal of a licence.

For certain types of products procedures must be established that control the use of and the settlement. An example would be derivatives. Procedures are needed for:

- Approval to deal in derivatives (general and specific products)
- Types of collateral accepted
- Closing out of positions
- Exercise, assignment and delivery

Stock lending agreements will also set out key procedures for the terms of the lend, the recall, lending rate, rebate rate, collateral and dealing with corporate actions. Critically important procedures will also exist for payments and transfer of funds to ensure not only the authorization but also the accuracy of the process.

Developing effective procedures is an important part of the Operations manager's role and they are clearly important in relation to efficiency, regulatory and risk management. We can also see that the correct documenting of procedures is also vital as is the regular reviewing and updating of the procedures. It is surprising how much change there is to procedures over even relatively short periods of time. A major change such as a new system will create procedural changes that are obvious and will prompt an update to take place. However, there are more subtle changes to both internal and external procedures that may be less obvious and the update of the documented procedures may be overlooked.

Managing procedures successfully will naturally lead to a more efficient and controlled Operations function. It is a challenge but nevertheless a crucial management role that is vital to the business.

Chapter 9

Industry initiatives

The introduction of many initiatives to combat risk over the years has led to a more efficient and uniform process and yet one that is by no means uniform across all countries. These initiatives include those set out by the Group of 30, an industry body that looked at issues surrounding the settlement of securities in the late 1980s. The International Securities Services Association (ISSA) later took on board the recommendations that they made, updated them and monitored markets to ascertain the extent of their implementation. Today we see many of the recommendations as standard practice in most, but not all, markets. The markets, of course, have undergone much change since the 1980s, including experiencing many 'disasters' and as a result the ISSA issued more recommendations in 2000 that sought to build on those of G30 and improve the whole settlement environment from the angles of both efficiency and risk. It is useful to look at the G30 and ISSA 2000 Recommendations not least because they are made by representatives from the industry, banks, brokers, etc. and therefore have credibility but also because they are often incorporated in some way into either regulation or best practice or both.

Group of 30 recommendations

1 All comparisons of trades between direct market participants (i.e. brokers, broker dealers and other exchange members) should be

accomplished by T+0. Matched trade details should be linked to the settlement system.

2 Indirect market participants (such as institutional investors, and other indirect trading counterparties) should achieve positive affirmation of trade details on T+1.
3 Each country should have in place an effective and fully developed central securities depository, organized and managed to encourage the broadest possible direct and indirect industry participation. The range of depository eligible instruments should be as wide as possible. Immobilization or dematerialization of financial instruments should be achieved to the utmost extent possible.
4 Each market is encouraged to reduce settlement risk by introducing either real-time gross settlement or a trade netting system that fully meets the 'Lamfalussy Recommendations'.
5 Delivery versus payment (DVP) should be employed as the method for settling all securities transactions. DVP is defined as follows: simultaneous, irrevocable and immediately available exchange of securities and cash on a continuous basis throughout the day.
6 Payments associated with the settlement of securities transactions and the servicing of securities portfolios should be made consistent across all instruments and markets by adopting the 'same day' funds convention.
7 A rolling settlement system should be adopted by all markets. Final settlement for all trades should occur no later than T+3.
8 Securities lending and borrowing should be encouraged as a method of expediting the settlement of securities transaction. Existing regulatory and taxation barriers that inhibit the practice of lending securities should be removed.
9 Each country should adopt the standard for securities messages developed by the International Organization of Standardization (ISO Standard 7775). In particular, countries should adopt the ISIN numbering system for securities issues as defined in the ISO Standard 6166.

Source: *Clearance & Settlement Systems in the World's Securities Markets*, G30 (1989) and updated by the ISSA (May 1995).

The ISSA Recommendations 2000 are:

1 Securities systems have a primary responsibility to their users and other stakeholders. They must provide effective low-cost processing. Services should be priced equitably.
2 Securities systems must allow the option of network access on an interactive basis. They should cope with peak capacity without any services degradation, and have sufficient standby capabilities to recover operations in a reasonably short period within each processing day.
3 The industry worldwide must satisfy the need for efficient, fast settlement by full adherence to the International Securities Numbering process (ISO 6166) and uniform usage of ISO 15022 standards for all securities messages. The industry should seek to introduce a global client and counterpart identification methodology (BIC – ISO 9362) to further facilitate straight-through processing. Applications and programmes should be structured in such a way as to facilitate open interaction between all parties.
4 Each market must have clear rules ensuring investor protection by safeguarding participants from the financial risks of failed settlement and that listed companies are required to follow sound policies on corporate governance, transfer of economic benefits and shareholder rights.
5 The major risks in securities systems should be mitigated by five key measures, namely:

- The implementation of real delivery versus payment
- The adoption of a trade date plus one settlement cycle in a form that does not increase operational risk
- The minimization of funding and liquidity constraints by enabling stock lending and borrowing, broad-based cross-collateralization, the use of repos and netting as appropriate
- The enforcement of scripless settlement
- The establishment of mandatory trade matching and settlement performance measures

6 Convergence of securities systems, both within countries and across borders, should be encouraged where this eliminates operational risk, reduces cost and enhances market efficiency.
7 Investor compliance with the laws and regulations in the home countries of their investments should be part of their regulators' due diligence process. Investors, in turn, should be treated equitably in the home country of their investments especially in respect to their rights to shareholder benefits and concessionary arrangements under double-tax agreements.
8 Local laws and regulations should ensure that there is segregation of client assets from the principal assets of their custodian; and no possible claim on client assets in the event of custodian bankruptcy or a similar event. Regulators and markets, to further improve investor protection, should work:

- To ensure clarity on the applicable law on cross-border transactions
- To seek international agreement on a legally enforceable definition of finality in a securities transaction
- To ensure that local law fully protects the rights of beneficial owners
- To strengthen securities laws both to secure the rights of the pledgee and the protection accorded to client assets held in securities systems

These recommendations are geared to improving efficiency and managing risk. Certain issues pertaining to clearing and settlement can have a significant impact on the efficiency of the whole process, and therefore on the efficiency and, of course, the risk of the market as a whole.

All participants in the industry have a responsibility to look at risk and assess how they contribute to it and how they are affected by it. This can be illustrated by the following statement:

> **Failure to adequately identify, evaluate and manage operational risks can expose the organisation, and the market itself, to financial loss . . .** (*Source: Global Custodian/Fall 1996; authors: Chris Thompson, Jeff Thompson and John Garvey*)

Note the reference to the systemic risk fear in the statement 'can expose the organisation and the market itself'.

The various initiatives mentioned in ISSA/G30 such as netting and stock lending are in their way processes for efficiency and risk reduction and operations managers will need to incorporate this into their controls and procedures.

In derivatives markets the Futures and Options Association issued an excellent overview of the risk facing end-users of derivatives. Published in 1995 and entitled *Managing Derivatives Risk – Guidelines for end-users of derivatives*, there were six core principles given in the guidelines. These can be summarized as:

1 Approval of an effective policy for the use of derivatives
2 Establish clear written procedures for implementing the derivatives policy
3 Activities should be subject to an effective framework of internal controls and audits
4 Establish a sound risk management function
5 Procedures for a full analysis of all credit risks
6 Procedures for monitoring legal risk

Of particular interest from the operations point of view is core principle 3. Here the guideline is that senior management should ensure that activities are in compliance with external regulations and internal policy, including procedures for the execution, confirmation, recording, processing and settlement of transactions. Among the suggested action points are:

- Carry out an independent review of internal controls operated to ensure that they comply with best practice
- Examine computer systems to ensure that they are adequate and robust and have been independently reviewed
- Ensure there are adequate controls over amendments to computer programs

These guidelines are another example of the industry providing help and advice to participants and it would not be difficult to incorporate these guidelines for securities business as well as derivatives.

Netting

As we have seen, the ISSA and other industry organizations have commented on how netting is a major source of risk reduction and can be part of the controls of a firm. In the exchange-traded derivative markets and now securities markets the clearing house in a central clearing counterparty arrangement usually operates on a netted settlement basis. Netting does, however, offer some problems for organizations that are acting in an agency capacity and also there are issues about the ability to enforce netting in cases of default. We mentioned earlier in the book how legal risk is an operational risk issue and clearly any doubts about the ability to enforce netting would constitute a legal/operational risk.

We should therefore familiarize ourselves with the issues surrounding netting and it is in the area of over-the-counter derivatives that netting can be best illustrated. To do this I would like to look at netting first in terms of what it is and then how agreements have been developed and utilized. The following extracts from a paper by Rudiger Litten of Norton Rose which looks at netting from a German point of view is an ideal case study for this purpose.

What is netting?

Netting is a method of reducing the exposure involved in a series of finance transactions by providing for the set-off of the mutual claims and obligations of the two parties concerned, so that only one single claim remains. There are three types of netting:

- **Payment (or settlement) netting:** The parties to one or a number of transactions agree that where payments must be made by each party at the same date and in the same currency, instead of the two amounts only a single net amount is to be paid, representing the difference between the two amounts. Payment netting usually takes place where there is an interest rate swap of the same currency and where, at a certain date, one party pays a fixed interest and the other a variable interest.
- **Novation netting:** Like payment netting, novation netting provides that the payments due from each party are netted so as to produce a single net sum on each settlement date and for each currency. Unlike payment netting, novation netting refers not only to the payments due under transactions but also to the transactions themselves. The transactions which give rise to the payment obligations are terminated and replaced by an agreement concerned only with the payment of the netted sum.
- **Close-out netting (liquidation-netting):** When an event of default occurs, all outstanding transactions between the parties terminate and a single sum becomes payable by one party to the other.

This article deals with close-out netting, as this type of netting has the most important practical implications.

Cherry picking

The purpose of close-out netting is to reduce the risk to which the parties involved in a series of transactions are exposed. In cases where there are a number of outstanding transactions between two parties and one party becomes insolvent, the receiver of the insolvent party has, in many jurisdictions, the right to disclaim the transactions he considers unprofitable while enforcing the others (this is called 'cherry picking'). Cherry picking is disadvantageous to the solvent party in two ways, as while it must pay the full amount in relation to the unprofitable transactions, it will probably only recover a fraction of its claims under the profitable contracts.

Furthermore, the receiver is not obliged to decide upon the future of the contracts immediately. Instead, he may conclude that some contracts which are currently unprofitable might become profitable in the future and may therefore disclaim them (or not as the case may be) at a later point in time. This makes it impossible for the other party to assess its position effectively.

It is often the case that the insolvency of one party leads to the insolvency of the other if cherry picking is not prevented. It is therefore in the interests of all parties involved to reduce their risks. This can be achieved by ensuring that, upon the insolvency of one party, all outstanding transactions are terminated and evaluated in accordance with some uniformly applicable principles. The results of such evaluations are then netted against each other, so that only one single lump sum remains payable by one of the parties.

Regulatory capital

An important consequence of such a netting regime is that, pursuant to the Basel Capital Accord and the EU Solvency Ratio Directive, the regulatory capital which a bank is required to hold against credit risks resulting from outstanding finance transactions is reduced.

Regulatory capital treatment of derivative transactions

The basis for regulatory capital in a large number of jurisdictions is the Basel Accord of 1988. Many Basel Accord proposals have found their way into the legislation of European states via various EU

Directives. The golden rule of capital adequacy is that the target standard ratio of regulatory capital to weighted risk assets is to be set at a minimum of 8%. With respect to risk assets such as loans, the weighting is comparatively easy. Under normal circumstances, the value of a loan against which regulatory capital must be held is the outstanding nominal amount of the loan. How are derivative transactions to be valued? The most common method is known as marking to market. Using this method, an amount is calculated which would have to be paid (or received) if the derivative transaction in question is terminated and replaced by an equivalent contract at current market rates. Such amount (plus, in most cases, a so-called add-on, covering a potential future risk increase) is then the basis against which the party, benefiting from the derivative transaction, is required to hold 8% regulatory capital.

The advantages of netting

Close-out netting has only relatively recently been recognized by the Basel Committee (and subsequently by European legislators) as having an effect on regulatory capital. It has, however, now been accepted that derivative transactions, concluded under an appropriate master agreement which provides for close-out netting, should be valued at an amount resulting from a set-off of all the derivative transactions plus the add-on covering a potential future risk increase. Thus, netting reduces the regulatory capital a bank is required to hold.

Criteria for netting agreements

In order to qualify for a reduction of regulatory capital, the transactions must be concluded under a bilateral master agreement that satisfies a number of criteria. The most important criteria are: the existence of a netting clause, pursuant to which, in the event of one party failing to perform due to default, bankruptcy or similar circumstances, a single legal obligation (covering all relevant transactions) is created so that the non-defaulting party has either a right to receive payments or an obligation to pay only the net sum of the positive and negative mark-to-market values of the relevant individual transactions. (The master agreement must not, however, contain a so-called 'walk-away-clause', i.e. a provision pursuant to which the non-defaulting party is only required to make part payments or no payments at all, if the netted amount turns out to be payable to the defaulting party.)

- The existence of a legal opinion, from external legal advisers, confirming the effectiveness of the netting agreement under:
  - The law of the country(s) in which the parties are incorporated
  - The law of the country(s) in which the branches of a party which are involved in the transactions, are located
  - The law governing the netting agreement and
- Procedures must be in place to ensure that the legal provisions of the netting agreement are kept under review in light of possible changes in the relevant laws.

Legal opinions

The ISDA has sponsored a number of legal opinions for the 1987 and 1992 master agreements. These legal opinions exist, *inter alia*, for all G10 states and they confirm that the netting provisions contained in the relevant master agreements are valid and enforceable. Similar legal opinions have been sponsored by a number of (national) banking associations with respect to various other master agreements, e.g. the French AFB and the German Deutscher Rahmenvertrag für Finanztermingeschäfte. If parties to a master agreement, for which a legal opinion has been given, intend to deviate from the wording of that agreement, they must ensure that any changes made do not render the legal opinion inapplicable.

Netting agreements

A number of master agreements contain netting provisions. Among these are:

- The ISDA Master Agreements of 1987 and 1992
- The European Master Agreement (EMA)
- The Master agreements sponsored by the British Bankers Association and the Foreign Exchange Committee of New York, such as:
  - Interbank Currency Options Market Master Agreement Terms (ICOM)
  - Interbank Foreign Exchange Master Agreement Terms (IFEMA)
  - Foreign Exchange and Options Master Agreement (FEOMA)
- The French 'Convention-Cadre AFB Relative aux Opérations de Marché à Terme'
- The Swiss 'Schweizer Rahmenvertrag für Over The Counter (OTC) Derivate' and
- The German 'Deutscher Rahmenvertrag für Finanztermingeschäfte'.

The majority of these master agreements do not contain a specific section which deals comprehensively with the netting issues and quite often the term 'netting' is not even used. Instead the master agreements contain a number of provisions which, when read together, provide for a netting system. These provisions (using the 1992 ISDA Master Agreement ('ISDA Master') and the (Deutscher) Rahmenvertrag für Finanztermingeschäfte ('DRF') as examples), are described below.

1992 ISDA Master Agreement

- Early termination of outstanding transactions Section 5(a)(1) ISDA Master provides for a number of events of default, including failure to pay or deliver and bankruptcy. If an event of default occurs in relation to one of the parties, the other may designate an Early Termination Date, or, in the case of bankruptcy, the parties may agree upon an Automatic Early Termination of all transactions.

- Consequences of early termination Following termination of the outstanding transactions, a lump sum amount (reflecting the value of all transactions) is calculated in accordance with a certain method previously agreed upon by the parties ('market quotation' or 'loss'). The parties must also agree whether a lump sum amount will be payable only to the non-defaulting party ('First Method' or 'One-way-payment') or whether the defaulting party will also be entitled to receive payment if, following calculation of the lump sum, it becomes apparent that the lump sum amount is in favour of the defaulting party ('Second Method' or 'Full-two-way-payments').

Deutscher Rahmenvertrag für Finanztermingeschäfte

- Early termination No. 7 DRF provides for the right to terminate all outstanding transactions upon 'good cause' (an example of 'good cause' is a party's failure to pay within five business days after notification) and for automatic termination of all transactions if one of the parties becomes 'insolvent'. 'Insolvency' in this context occurs when a justifiable application for opening insolvency proceedings is filed. The consequence of early termination is that the mutual claims of the parties cease to exist and are replaced by compensation claims.
- Compensation Following early termination of all outstanding transactions, a compensation claim for each transaction will be calculated on the basis of methods which do not, in principle, differ from the methods offered under the ISDA Master.
- Final payment The compensation claims for all transactions will be netted with each other and with any further claims the parties may have against each other. As a result, there will only be one single lump sum payable by one party to the other.

Source: 'An Introduction to Netting from a German Law Perspective', *Rüdiger Litten* and *Norton Rose*, 4 January 2002 by kind permission from gtnews, *www.gtnews.com*

There are many issues surrounding netting as the above shows, and indeed some of the other initiatives proposed and taking place in the industry are not as straightforward as Operations managers and teams might like.

Shortening settlement cycles and the central clearing counterparty will reduce risk from the failed settlement but will increase pressures within the operations function and industry structure to ensure settlement can take place on due date. Likewise STP projects remove mainly manual and capacity risks but replace them with system risk.

Other initiatives such as requiring Operations personnel to be qualified to a recognized industry standard will help to raise even further the professionalism in Operations, which in turn should have a positive knock-on effect in the industry in general. The industry and its participants are constantly looking for ways and means to improve the workings of the markets and support structures and within the participating organizations as well. Anyone working within the Operations environment and most certainly those at supervisor or manager level must ensure that they are aware of these initiatives and, more importantly, where they can they contribute to the development and introduction of initiatives.

My final comment on controls, procedures and risk concerns knowledge. People are an organization's greatest asset and their knowledge is a key factor in this. An example of a comprehensive glossary of terms appears at the end of this book and a good question to consider is this – would your team of people know the meaning of all or most of the terms in the glossary?

If the answer is yes, then the knowledge factor is high. The primary control process is already in place, now how do you build on it and manage risk?

Appendix 1

Relevant website addresses

Australia

ASX – Australian Stock Exchange	www.asx.com.au
SFE – Sydney Futures Exchange	www.sfe.com.au
Australian Financial Markets Association	www.afma.com

Belgium

Brussels Exchanges	www.bxs.be

Brazil

BM&F – Bolsa De Mercadorias and Futuros	www.bmf.com.br
Sao Paulo Stock Exchange	www.bvrj.com.br

Canada

ME – Montreal Exchange	www.me.org
TFE – Toronto Futures Exchange	www.tse.com
VSE – Vancouver Stock Exchange	www.vse.ca
WCE – Winnipeg Commodity Exchange	www.wce.ca

China

SME – Shanghai Metal Exchange	www.shme.com

Denmark

FUTOP – Guarantee Fund for Danish Futures and Options	www.xcse.dk

Finland

FOEX – The Finnish Options Exchange	www.foex.fi
SOM – Finnish Securities and Derivatives Exchange	www.som.fi

France

MATIF – Marche à Terme International de France	www.matif.fr
MONEP – Marche des Options Negotiables de Paris	www.monep.fr

Germany

Hannover Commodity Exchange	www.wtb-hannover.de
Eurex	www.eurexchange.com

Hong Kong

HKEX – Hong Kong Exchanges & Clearing Ltd	www.hkex.com.hk

Hungary

BCE – Budapest Commodity Exchange	www.bce-bat.com
BSE – Budapest Stock Exchange	www.bse.hu

Israel

Tel Aviv Stock Exchange	www.tase.co.il

India

National Stock Exchange of India	www.nseindia.com

Italy

IDEM – Italian Derivatives Market	www.idem.it

Japan

Hanmon Commodity Exchange	www.hce.or.jp
OSE – Osaka Securities Exchange	quote.ose.or.jp (not www.)

TCE – Tokyo Commodity Exchange	www.tocom.or.jp
TGE – Tokyo Grain Exchange	www.tge.or.jp
TIFFE – Tokyo International Financial Futures Exchange	www.tiffe.or.jp
TSE – Tokyo Stock Exchange	www.tse.or.jp

Korea

Korea Stock Exchange	www.kse.or.kr

Malaysia

KLCE – Kuala Lumpur Commodity Exchange	www.klce.com.my
Commodity and Monetary Exchange of Malaysia	commex.com.my

Netherlands

EURONEXT	www.euronext.com

New Zealand

NZFOE – New Zealand Futures & Options Exchange	www.sfe.com.au

Norway

Oslo Stock Exchangc	www.ose.no/english/

Portugal

BDP – Bolsa de Derivados de Porto	www.bdp.pt

Russia

The Russian Exchange	www.re.ru

Singapore

Singapore Commodity Exchange	www.sicom.com.sg
Singapore Exchange	www.sgx.com

South Africa

SAFEX – South African Futures Exchange	www.safex.co.za
JSE – Johannesburg Stock Exchange	www.jse.co.za

Spain

MEFF	www.meff.es

Sweden

OM Stockholmbörsen	www.stockholmborsen.se

Switzerland

EUREX	www.eurexchange.com

Turkey

Istanbul Stock Exchange	www.ise.org

United Kingdom

IPE – International Petroleum Exchange	www.ipe.uk.com
LIFFE – London International Financial Futures & Options Exchange	www.liffe.com
LME – London Metal Exchange	www.lme.co.uk
OMLX – The London Securities & Derivatives Exchange	www.stockholmborsen.se

United States of America

AMEX – American Stock Exchange	www.amex.com
CBOE – Chicago Board Options Exchange	www.cboe.com
CBOT – Chicago Board of Trade	www.cbot.com
CME – Chicago Mercantile Exchange	www.cme.com
CSCE – Coffee, Sugar & Cocoa Exchange Inc.	www.csce.com
KCBT – Kansas City Board of Trade	www.kcbt.com
MGE – Minneapolis Grain Exchange	www.mgex.com

NYBOT – New York Board of Trade	www.nybot.com
NYCE – New York Cotton Exchange	www.nyce.com
NYMEX – New York Mercantile Exchange	www.nymex.com
NYSE – New York Stock Exchange	www.nyse.com
PHLX – Philadelphia Stock Exchange	www.phlx.com
NASDAQ	www.nasdaq.com

Bank for International Settlement www.bis.org
(for information on the Basel Capital Accord)

Appendix 2

Operational risk – moving forward

With thanks to FOW and AFMA

Risk managers, CEOS and treasury executives across the world are concluding that the management of operational risk delivers substantial benefits to a company's bottom line and shareholder value. Unfortunately this link is still often underestimated, resulting in substantial reputation damage and/or financial loss.

If market and credit risk were the buzz phrases of the 1990s, operational risk is definitely the topic of this decade. One only has to look at the priorities of industry regulators and the increasing presence within treasury of operational risk resources to understand the attention this issue is attracting.

For example, in the UK, the British Bankers' Association (BBA) has published a discussion paper on operational risk, designed to lay the groundwork for further debate on industry operational risk management practices and the development of regulatory policy. The Association is also working on a database of operational risk incidents, which it hopes will help the industry monitor and manage operational risk. In the US, operational risk management has been the subject of Federal Reserve Board discussions and research papers. In addition, the Bank for International Settlements (BIS) has recently covered operational risk in new guidelines on risk management.

Meanwhile, industry bodies in Australia – the Australian Financial Markets Association (AFMA) and the Australian Treasury Operations Association (ATOA) – partnered consulting firm Arthur Andersen to produce a definition of operational risk and deliver a standard that Australian financial institutions are enthusiastically adopting to identify and manage operational risk. This paper defines operational 'best practice' standards and is known as SCOR – Standards for the Control of Operational Risk.

SCOR is a blueprint for operational risk management. Launched late last year, it has been adopted by 30 institutions in Australia, with an additional 25 taking it under consideration. SCOR offers financial institutions an operational risk management framework and reference tool, covering financial markets such as foreign exchange, cash and discount securities, fixed interest and repurchase agreements. Unsurprisingly, its application has not been limited to these five markets, with uptake from institutions trading in areas such as derivatives (including electricity), exchange-traded futures and equities.

Australian industry associations representing corporate interests have also shown strong interest in SCOR on behalf of their members, with SCOR featured in member seminars and focus group discussions. Several state-based treasury corporations are in the process of assessing SCOR with two already on board as users. Several electricity corporations are also using SCOR.

It is the intention of AFMA and ATOA to expand SCOR to cover additional product areas and to convert SCOR to electronic form. Australian SCOR users have encouraged this with strong interest also being shown by overseas-based organizations. In addition, AFMA and ATOA intend to promote the SCOR operational risk initiative to other global centres for financial services.

'The big thing about SCOR is that it was the industry itself that initiated the concept,' explains Ken Farrow, chief executive of

AFMA. 'Over the space of 12 months, representatives from over 30 financial institutions voluntarily shared experiences that, with the guidance of the industry associations and Arthur Andersen, was complied and developed into an industry standard.'

Breakdown

A breakdown in operational risk management can lead to poor use of resources: for example, management becoming embroiled in dispute resolution over poorly executed trading contracts. Alternatively, major losses may occur, as in the recent cases of Daiwa and Barings.

The successful management of operational risk is about identifying, managing and containing operational risk factors and developing operational risk mitigation strategies to reduce the potential for unanticipated financial loss as a result of weaknesses in the control framework.

When operational risk is managed effectively, earnings volatility and costs are also reduced. AFMA and ATOA believe SCOR will reduce exposure to risk, provide a platform for best practice standards, reduce error rates, provide common standards, improve efficiencies and reduce audit costs.

'But don't take our word for it, check with the market,' says Peter Cannizzaro, chairman of ATOA. Cannizzaro, like AFMA's Farrow, emphasises that SCOR is industry-prepared and driven, with a large number of Australian and international institutions taking part in its preparation and uptake. 'This not only makes it relevant to the industry, but practical and on target with industry needs,' he adds.

With the development of SCOR, the Australian financial market is working with the local regulator Australian Prudential Regulation

Authority (APRA) toward better management of operational risk. Having taken the initiative, the industry argues it is sharing this goal with APRA, but from a self-regulatory perspective.

Structure

SCOR defines the content of the risk management process and outlines practical implications within a treasury environment. It provides a structure and terminology that aims to standardize risk management procedures and terminology with reference to operational risk matters (see diagram overleaf). If your organization is SCOR-compliant, counterparties know that effective levels of operational risk management are in place.

For ease of application, SCOR is divided into two sections. The first part of the document provides general and specific controls and is a quick reference and audit tool. Specific controls relate to specific process flows, such as reconciliation, settlement or confirmation. General controls relate to every process. Detailed descriptions of each control are provided.

The second part of the document examines the processes used to manage operational risk. It highlights operational risk categories, risk objectives and control procedures. Each control standard, risk and process is extensively cross-referenced throughout the document.

AFMA and ATOA state that SCOR should be used to support:

- establishment of a risk management process within treasury operations;
- evaluation of the risk management process;
- identification of areas of potential risk – the evaluation of the control environment;
- identification of additional controls to be implemented within an organization.

Controls are described in terms of minimum or recommended standards set by the industry for the successful management of operational risk. In order to remain relevant to the marketplace, given the speed with which the industry changes, SCOR does not identify all controls that might be necessary to manage operational risk, within the tolerance levels set by an organization. To do so would inhibit industry development, which would in turn result in a failure to meet operational risk management objectives.

Practical application

The following case, which involved the electricity derivatives industry, highlights several incidents of operational risk management failure. The case itself attracted so much attention in Australia that at one stage, it was thought it would be the sole reason for the state government of New South Wales' refusal to deregulate the New South Wales power industry.

The case concerns a dispute between Victorian power retailer Powercor Australia and Pacific Power (owned by the state government of New South Wales).

Powercor alleged that between 13 November 1997 and 11 June 1998 the parties entered into eleven electricity derivatives contracts (nine two-way swaps and two cap contracts) under the Isda master agreement and sought specific performance of those contracts. There was no confirmation signed in respect of any of the eleven disputed contracts.

Pacific Power submitted that there was no concluded and binding contract with regard to the eleven disputed contracts because;

- it was the common intention of the parties that no binding contract would come into existence until a confirmation was signed and exchanged;

- the parties had not reached agreement on the essential terms of each transaction and many of the terms were incomplete and/or uncertain;
- the parties had not, therefore, reached the stage where they intended to be bound; and
- the employees of Pacific Power and Powercor who negotiated the disputed transactions did not have the authority to enter into the contracts.

Pacific Power also raised issues of mistake and counterclaimed for misrepresentation under sections 52 and 53 of the Trade Practices Act (Commonwealth) 1974.

The judge held that the eleven disputed transactions were final and binding contracts, even though relevant confirmations had not been signed and exchanged, stating, among other things, that:

- The master agreement sets out the terms upon which the parties agree to negotiate and provides for the time when a contract comes into being.
- A contract comes into existence at the time the parties agree the essential terms of the transaction.
- The confirmation is no more than a record of the contract previously made.
- The pattern of dealings between parties could vary that general position under the master agreement if those dealings provide clear and unequivocal evidence that no transactions under the master agreement will be binding until a signed confirmation is exchanged. In this case, the judge held that the failure to sign and exchange confirmations did not establish a lack of intention to contract.

In December 1999, the judge ordered that the eleven disputed contracts governed by the Isda master agreement be specifically performed. The Supreme Court of Victoria ordered Pacific Power to pay Powercor A$44.7 m for money owed on hedging contracts that were in dispute. Pacific Power was also ordered to a pay an additional

A$3.15m in costs to Powercor. An appeal against the decision has been lodged by Pacific Power and is listed to commence on 2 October 2000.

A number of operational risk management failures led to the court action. There was no confirmation signed in relation to the eleven disputed contracts and it was alleged that the employees of Pacific Power and Powercor who negotiated the disputed contracts did not have the authority to enter into the contracts. Furthermore, one party's position was considerably strengthened because it maintained scrupulous records of the transactions, while the judge stated that an *ad hoc* system of record keeping undermined the second party to the case.

Standards

Although SCOR has been written for five OTC markets, namely foreign exchange, cash and discount securities, fixed interest and repurchase agreements, its application in any treasury environment would ensure a high level of operational risk management compliance.

The standard clearly outlines a process for monitoring and managing controls, beginning with staff training, and continuing on to documentation, model implementation, resources, regulatory compliance, review of market practices, deal ticket completion and collection, standard confirmation format and non-standard settlement instructions. Settlement checking and authorization controls are listed, along with more than 100 other control factors, as a minimum requirement.

Settlement authorization involves obtaining an authority from the appropriate personnel for settlement of deals where the client/counterparty confirmation is not received by cut-off time. Being able to put a tick in the box confirming that this has taken place means that one minor incident of operational risk failure may be avoided. It may also mean that management time is not diverted into sorting out poorly executed trades, which could later land either or both parties in court.

SCOR's comprehensive list of controls is supported by a process outline. It defines the elements of managing operational risk as organizational strategy and culture; risk management infrastructure; risk identification and risk assessment; control evaluation; risk treatment; reporting and communicating; monitoring and improvement. This is closely aligned with an approach taken by the BBA, which lists strategy, risk policy, risk management process, risk mitigation, operations management and culture in its enterprise-wide operational risk management framework.

Figure A2.1 The process of managing operational risk (*Source*: SCOR)

Much attention is paid in SCOR to process flows, from deal preparation and entry to confirmation, settlement, reconciliation and exception management. For example, the document examines the individual risks or group of risks that could arise as the result of a new counterparty or client relationship. These risks include: failure to capture all information, as a result of the client using different forms for standard settlement instructions; incomplete information, resulting from staff failure in completing standard new client forms; business being transacted with the client prior to the establishment of an operational system; and the misfiling of counterparty documents. Group risks include information supporting the establishment of a new client being incomplete, inaccurate, unauthorized and untimely.

The risks appear mundane and minute, but without a comprehensive set of reference tools to check and countercheck, the smallest error may later lead to inappropriate use of resources, as in the Pacific Power vs Powercor case, or, in the case of unauthorized trading, a Barings-style collapse.

AFMA and ATOA believe the best course of action for treasury operators is self-regulation. SCOR provides a detailed framework for organizations to monitor and manage their own operational risk, on a level that is on par with the management of credit risk. Industry participants worldwide should aim for best practice. Best practice implemented via SCOR may reduce the likelihood of large-scale losses and prevent smaller incidents.

Sharon Murray, head of sales, marketing and communications; Gerg Wrate, manager policy and research; Ingrid Fabian, account executive, SCOR, at the Australian Financial Markets Association.

Case details on Powercor Australia Limited vs Public Power prepared by Andrew Booth, partner, Freehills

Glossary

30/360 Also 360/360 or 30(E)/360. A day/year count convention assuming 30 days in each calendar month and a 'year' of 360 days; adjusted in America for certain periods ending on 31st-day of the month (and then sometimes known as 30(A)/360).

AAA The highest credit rating for a company or asset – the risk of default is negligible.

Accrued interest Interest due on a bond or other fixed income security that must be paid by the buyer of a security to its seller. Usual compensation: coupon rate of interest times elapsed days from prior interest payment date (i.e. coupon date) up to but not including settlement date.

Actual settlement date Date the transaction effectively settles in the clearing house (exchange of securities eventually against cash).

Add-on In capital adequacy calculations, the extra capital required to allow for the possibility of a deal moving into profit before a mark-to-market calculation is next made.

Affirmation Affirmation refers to the counterparty's agreement with the terms of the trade as communicated.

Agent One who executes orders for or otherwise acts on behalf of another (the principal) and is subject to its control and authority. The agent takes no financial risk and may receive a fee or commission.

Agent bank A commercial bank that provides services as per their instructions.

Allocation (give up) The process of moving the trade from the executing broker to the clearing broker in exchange-traded derivatives.

Amortization Accounting procedure that gradually reduces the cost value of a limited life asset or intangible asset through periodic charges to income. The purpose of amortization is to reflect the resale or redemption value. Amortization also refers to the reduction of debt by regular payments of interest and principal to pay off a loan by maturity.

Annuity For the recipient, an arrangement whereby the individual receives a pre-specified payment annually for a pre-specified number of years.

Ask price Price at which a market-maker will sell stock. Also known as the offer price.

Assets Everything of value that is owned or is due: fixed assets (cash, buildings and machinery) and intangible assets (patents and goodwill).

Assignment The process by which the holder of a short option position is matched against a holder of a similar long option position who has exercised his right.

Authentication agent A bank putting a signature on each physical bond to certify its genuineness prior to the distribution of the definitive bonds on the market.

Bank of England The UK's central bank which undertakes policy decided by the Treasury and determines interest rates.

Bankers' acceptance Short-term negotiable discount note, drawn on and accepted by banks which are obliged to pay the face value amount at maturity.

Bargain Another word for a transaction or deal. It does not imply that a particularly favourable price was obtained.

Base currency Currency chosen for reporting purposes.

Basis (gross) The difference between the relevant cash instrument price and the futures price. Often used in the context of hedging the cash instrument.

Basis (value or net) The difference between the gross basis and the carry.

Basis point (BP) A change in the interest rate of one hundredth of one per cent (0.01%). One basis point is written as 0.01 when 1.0 represents 1%.

Basis risk The risk that the price or rate of one instrument or position might not move exactly in line with the price or rate of another instrument or position which is being used to hedge it.

BBA British Bankers' Association.

Bear Investor who believes prices will fall.

Bearer document Documents which state on them that the person in physical possession (the bearer) is the owner.

Benchmark bond The most recently issued and most liquid government bond.

Beneficial owner The underlying owner of a security who has paid for the stock and is entitled to the benefits of ownership.

Bid (a) The price or yield at which a purchaser is willing to buy a given security. (b) To quote a price or yield at which a purchaser is able to buy a given security.

Bilateral netting A netting system in which all trades executed on the same date in the same security between the same counterparties are grouped and netted to one final delivery versus payment.

Bill of exchange A money market instrument.

BIS Bank for International Settlements.

Block trade A purchase or sale of a large number of shares or dollar value of bonds normally much more than what constitutes a round lot in the market in question.

Bond A certificate of debt, generally long-term, under the terms of which an issuer contracts, *inter alia*, to pay the holder a fixed principal amount on a stated future date and, usually, a series of interest payments during its life.

Bonus issue A free issue of shares to a company's existing shareholders. No money changes hands and the share price falls pro rata. It is a cosmetic exercise to make the shares more marketable. Also known as a capitalization or scrip issue.

Book entry transfer System of recording ownership of securities by computer where the owners do not receive a certificate. Records are kept (and altered) centrally in 'the book'.

Books closed day Last date for the registration of shares or bonds for the payment of the next.

Break A term used for any out-of-balance condition. A money break means that debits and credits are not equal. A trade break means that some information such as that from a contra broker is missing to complete that trade.

Broker/dealer Any member firm of the Stock Exchange except the specialists which are GEMMs and IDBs.

Broken date A maturity date other than the standard ones normally quoted.

Broken period A period other than the standard ones normally quoted.

Broking The activity of representing a client as agent and charging commission for doing so.

Bull Investor who believes prices will rise.

Buying in The action taken by a broker failing to receive delivery of securities from a counterparty on settlement date to purchase these securities in the open market.

Call deposits Deposits which can be called (or withdrawn) at the option of the lender (and in some cases the borrower) after a specified period. The period is short, usually one or two days, and interest is paid at prevailing short-term rates (call account).

Call option An option that gives the seller the right, but not the obligation, to buy a specified quantity of the underlying asset at a fixed price, on or before a specified date. The buyer of a call option has the obligation (because they have bought the right) to make delivery of the underlying asset if the option is exercised by the seller.

Callable bond A bond that the issuer has the right to redeem prior to maturity by paying some specified call price.

Capital adequacy Requirement for firms conducting investment business to have sufficient funds.

Capital markets A term used to describe the means by which large amounts of money (capital) are raised by companies, governments and other organizations for long-term use and the subsequent trading of the instruments issued in recognition of such capital.

Capitalization issue *See* **Bonus issues**.

CASCADE Name of the settlement system used by Clearstream for German equity settlement.

Cash market A term used to describe the market where the cash asset trades, or the underlying market when talking about derivatives.

Cash sale A transaction on the floor of the stock exchange which calls for delivery of the securities that same day. In 'regular way' trades, the seller delivers securities on the fifth business day.

Cash settlement In the money market a transaction is said to be made for cash settlement if the securities purchased are delivered against payment on the same day the trade is made.

Central securities depository An organization which holds securities in either immobilized or dematerialized form thereby enabling transactions to be processed by book entry transfer. Also provides securities administration services.

Certificate of deposit A money market instrument.

CFTC The Commodities and Futures Commission, (United States).

Chaps Clearing House Automated Payment System – clearing system for sterling and Euro payments between banks.

Cheapest to deliver The cash security that provides the lowest cost (largest profit) to the arbitrage trader; the cheapest to deliver instrument is used to price the futures contract.

Clean price The total price of a bond less accrued interest.

Clearance The process of determining accountability for the exchange of money and securities between counterparties to a trade: clearance creates statements of obligation for securities and/or funds due.

Clearance broker A broker who will handle the settlement of securities related transactions for himself or another broker. Sometimes small brokerage firms may not clear for themselves and therefore employ the services of an outside clearing broker.

Clearing The centralized process whereby transacted business is recorded and positions are maintained.

Clearing house Company that acts as central counterparty for the settlement of stock exchange transactions. For example, on TD,

Broker X sold 100, 300 and 500 securities ABC and purchased 50 and 200 units of the same issue. The clearing system will net the transactions and debit X with 650 units (–900 + 250 = 650) against the total cash amount. This enables reduction of the number of movements and thus the costs.

Clearing organization The clearing organization acts as the guarantor of the performance and settlement of contracts that are traded on an exchange.

Clearing system System established to clear transactions.

Clearstream CSD and clearing house based in Luxembourg and Frankfurt.

Closing day In a new bond issue, the day when securities are delivered against payment by syndicate members participating in the offering.

Closing trade A bought or sold trade which is used to partly offset an open position, to reduce it or to fully offset it and close it.

CMO Central Moneymarkets Office – clearing house and depository for UK money markets.

Collateral An acceptable asset used to cover a margin requirement.

Commercial paper A money market instrument.

Commission Charge levied by a firm for agency broking.

Commodity futures These comprise five main categories; agricultural (e.g. wheat and potatoes), softs (e.g. coffee and cocoa), precious metals (e.g. gold and silver), non-ferrous metals (e.g. copper and lead), and energies (e.g. oil and gas).

Common stock Securities which represent ownership in a corporation. The two most important common stockholder rights are the voting right and dividend right. Common stockholder's claims on corporate assets are subordinate to those of bondholders preferred stockholders and general creditors.

Compliance officer Person appointed within an authorized firm to be responsible for ensuring compliance with the rules.

Compound interest Interest calculated on the assumption that interest amounts will be received periodically and can be reinvested (usually at the same rate).

Conduct of Business Rules Rules required by FSA 1986 to dictate how firms conduct their business. They deal mainly with the relationship between firm and client.

Conflicts of interest Circumstances that arise where a firm has an investment which could encourage it not to treat its clients favourably. The more areas in which a firm is involved, the greater the number of potential conflicts.

Confirm An agreement for each individual OTC transaction which has specific terms.

Continuous net settlement Extends multilateral netting to handle failed trades brought forward. *See* ***Multilateral netting***.

Contract The standard unit of trading for futures and options. It is also commonly referred to as a 'lot'.

Contract for difference Contract designed to make a profit or avoid a loss by reference to movements in the price of an item. The underlying item cannot change hands.

Contract note Legal documentation sent by securities house to clients providing details of a transaction completed on their behalf.

Conversion premium The effective extra cost of buying shares through exercising a convertible bond compared with buying the shares directly in the market. Usually expressed as percentage of the current market price of the shares.

Conversion price The normal value of a convertible which may be exchanged for one share.

Conversion ratio The number of shares into which a given amount (e.g. £100 or $1000) of the nominal value of a convertible can be converted.

Convertible bond Security (usually a bond or preferred stock) that can be exchanged for other securities, usually common stock of the same issuer, at the option of the holder and under certain conditions.

Convertible currency A currency that is freely convertible into another currency. Currencies for which domestic exchange control legislation specifically allows conversion into other currencies.

Corporate action One of many possible capital restructuring changes or similar actions taken by the company, which may have an impact on the market price of its securities, and which may require the shareholders to make certain decisions.

Corporate debt securities Bonds or commercial papers issued by private corporations.

Correlation Refers to the degree to which fluctuations of one variable are similar to those of another.

Cost of carry The net running cost of holding a position (which may be negative), e.g. the cost of borrowing cash to buy a bond, less the coupon earned on the bond while holding it.

Counterparty A trade can take place between two or more counterparties. Usually one party to a trade refers to its trading partners as counterparties.

Coupon Generally, the nominal annual rate of interest expressed as a percentage of the principal value. The interest is paid to the holder of a fixed income security by the borrower. The coupon is generally paid annually, semi-annually or, in some cases quarterly depending on the type of security.

Credit risk The risk that a borrower, or a counterparty to a deal, or the issuer of a security, will default on repayment or not deliver its side of the deal.

CREST The organization in the UK that holds UK and Irish company shares in dematerialized form and clears and settles trades in UK and Irish company shares.

CRESTCo Organization which owns CREST.

CREST member A participant within CREST who holds stock in stock accounts in CREST and whose name appears on the share register. A member is their own *user*.

CREST sponsored member A participant within CREST who holds stock in stock accounts in CREST and whose name appears on the share register. Unlike a member, a sponsored member is not their own user. The link to CREST is provided by another user who sponsors the sponsored member.

CREST user A participant within CREST who has an electronic link to CREST.

Cross-border trading Trading which takes place between persons or entities from different countries.

Cum-dividend With dividend.

Cumulative preference share If the company fails to pay a preference dividend the entitlement to the dividend accumulates and the arrears of preference dividend must be paid before any ordinary dividend.

Currency exposure Currency exposure exists if assets are held or income earned, in one currency while liabilities are denominated in another currency. The position is exposed to changes in the relative values of the two currencies such that the cost of the liabilities may be increased or the value of the assets or earning decreased.

CUSIP The committee on Uniform Securities Identification Procedures, the body which established a consistent securities numbering system in the United States.

Custodian Institution holding securities in safekeeping for a client. A custodian also offers different services to its clients (settlement, portfolio services, etc.).

Customer-non-private Customer who is assumed to understand the workings of the investment world and therefore receives little protection from the Conduct of Business Rules.

Customer-private Customer who is assumed to be financially unsophisticated and therefore receives more protection from the Conduct of Business Rules.

Day count fraction The proportion of a year by which an interest rate is multiplied in order to calculate the amount accrued or payable.

Dealer Individual or firm that acts as principal in all transactions, buying for their own account.

Default Failure to perform on a futures contract, either cash settlement or physical settlement.

Deliverable basket The list of securities which meets the delivery standards of futures contracts.

Delivery The physical movement of the underlying asset on which the derivative is based from seller to buyer.

Delivery versus payment Settlement where transfer of the security and payment for that security occur simultaneously.

Dematerialized (form) Circumstances where securities are held in a book entry transfer system with no certificates.

Depository receipts Certificate issued by a bank in a country to represent shares of a foreign corporation issued in a foreign country. It entitles the holder to dividends and capital gains. They trade and pay dividend in the currency of the country of issuance of the certificate.

Depository Trust Company (DTC) A US central securities depository through which members may arrange deliveries of securities between each other through electronic debit and credit entries without the physical delivery of the securities. DTC is industry-owned with the NYSE as the majority owner and is a member of the Federal Reserve System.

Derivative A financial instrument whose value is dependent upon the value of an underlying asset.

Dirty price The total price of a bond including accrued interest.

Disclaimer A notice or statement intending to limit or avoid potential legal liability.

Deutsche Börse The German Stock Exchange.

Dividend Distribution of profits made by a company if it chooses to do so.

Dividend per share Indicated annual dividend based on the most recently announced quarterly dividend times four plus any additional dividends to be paid during the current fiscal year.

Dividend yield The dividend expressed as a percentage of the share price.

DK Don't Know. Applies to a securities transaction pending settlement where fundamental data are missing which prevents the receiving party from accepting delivery.

Domestic bond Bond issued in the country of the issuer, in its country and according to the regulations of that country.

DTC Depository Trust Company – CSD for shares in the USA.

ECB European Central Bank.

ECSDA European Central Securities Depository Association.

EFP Exchange of futures for physical. Common in the energy markets. A physical deal priced on the futures markets.

EUCLID Communications system operated by Euroclear.

EUREX German–Swiss derivatives exchange created by the merger of the German (DTB) and Swiss (SOFFEX) exchanges.

EURONEXT A Pan-European exchange incorporating the Dutch, French and Belgium Exchanges and Liffe.

Earnings per share (EPS) The total profit of a company divided by the number of shares in issue.

Equity A common term to describe stocks or shares.

Equity/stock options Contracts based on individual equities or shares. On exercise of the option the specified amount of shares are exchanged between the buyer and the seller through the clearing organization.

E-T-D This is the common term which is used to describe exchange-traded derivatives which are the standardized products. It also differentiates products which are listed on an exchange as opposed to those offered Over-The-Counter.

EURIBOR A measure of the average cost of funds over the whole euro area based on a panel of 57 banks.

Eurobond An interest-bearing security issued across national borders, usually issued in a currency other than that of the issuer's home country.

Euroclear A book-entry clearing facility for most Eurocurrency and foreign securities. It is linked to EURONEXT.

European style option An option which can only be exercised on the expiry day.

Exception-based processing Transaction processing where straightforward items are processed automatically, allowing staff to concentrate on the items which are incorrect or not straightforward.

Execution and clearing agreement An agreement signed between the client and the clearing broker. This agreement sets out the terms by which the clearing broker will conduct business with the client.

Exchange Marketplace for trading.

Exchange delivery settlement price (EDSP) The price determined by the exchange for physical delivery of the underlying instrument or cash settlement.

Exchange-owned clearing organization Exchange- or member-owned clearing organizations are structured so that the clearing members each guarantee each other with the use of a members' default fund and additional funding such as insurance, with no independent guarantee.

Exchange rate The rate at which one currency can be exchanged for another.

Ex-date Date on or after which a sale of securities is executed without the right to receive dividends or other entitlements.

Ex-dividend Thirty-seven days before interest payment is due gilt-edged stocks are made 'ex-dividend'. After a stock has become 'ex-dividend', a buyer of stock purchases it without the right to receive the next (pending) interest payment.

Execution The action of trading in the markets.

Execution and clearing agreement An agreement signed between the client and the clearing broker. This sets out the terms by which the clearing broker will conduct business with the client.

Execution only or give-up agreement Tripartite agreement which is signed by the executing broker, the clearing broker and the client. This sets out the terms by which the clearing broker will accept business on behalf of the client.

Exercise The process by which the holder of an option may take up their right to buy or sell the underlying asset.

Exercise price (or strike price) The fixed price, per share or unit, at which an option conveys the right to call (purchase) or put (sell) the underlying shares or units.

Expiry date The last date on which an option holder can exercise their right. After this date an option is deemed to lapse or be abandoned.

Face value The value of a bond, note, mortgage or other security that appears on the face of the issue, unless the value is otherwise specified by the issuing company. Face value is ordinarily the amount the issuing company promises to pay at maturity. It is also referred to as par or nominal value.

Failed transaction A securities transaction that does not settle on time; i.e. the securities and/or cash are not exchanged as agreed on the settlement date.

Final settlement The completion of a transaction when the delivery of all components of a trade is performed.

Financial futures/options contracts Financial futures is a term used to describe futures contracts based on financial instruments such as currencies, debt instruments and financial indices.

Financial Services Authority (FSA) The agency designated by the Treasury to regulate investment business as required by FSA 1986 and then FSMA 2000. It is the main regulator of the financial sector and was formerly called the Securities and Investments Board (SIB). It assumed its full powers on 1 December 2001.

First notice day The first day that the holders of short positions can give notification to the exchange/clearing house that they wish to effect delivery.

Fiscal agent A commercial bank appointed by the borrower to undertake certain duties related to the new issue, such as assisting the payment of interest and principal, redeeming bonds or coupons, handling taxes, replacement of lost or damaged securities, destruction of coupons and bonds once payments have been made.

Fixed income Interest on a security which is calculated as a constant specified percentage of the principal amount and paid at the end of specified interest periods, usually annually or semi-annually, until maturity.

Fixed rate A borrowing or investment where the interest or coupon paid is fixed throughout the arrangement. In a FRA or coupon swap, the fixed rate is the fixed interest rate paid by one party to the other, in return for a floating-rate receipt (i.e. an interest rate that is to be refixed at some future time or times).

Fixed-rate borrowing This establishes the interest rate that will be paid throughout the life of the loan.

Flat position A position which has been fully closed out and no liability to make or take delivery exists.

Floating rate A borrowing or investment where the interest or coupon paid changes throughout the arrangement in line with some reference rate such as LIBOR. In a FRA or coupon swap, the floating rate is the floating interest rate (i.e. an interest rate that is to be refixed at some future time or times) paid by one party to the other, in return for a fixed-rate receipt.

Floating-rate note (FRN) Bond where each interest payment is made at the current or average market levels, often by reference to LIBOR.

Foreign bond Bond issued in a domestic market in the domestic currency and under the domestic rules of issuance by a foreign issuer (ex. Samurai bonds are bonds issued by issuers of other countries on the Japanese market).

Forex Abbreviation for foreign exchange (currency trading).

Forward delivery Transactions which involve a delivery date in the future.

Forward-rate agreements (FRAs) An agreement where the client can fix the rate of interest that will be applied to a notional loan or deposit, drawn or placed on an agreed date in the future, for a specified term.

Forwards These are very similar to futures contracts but they are not mainly traded on an exchange. They are not marked to market daily but settled only on the delivery date.

FSA Financial Services Authority.

FT-SE 100 index Main UK share index based on 100 leading shares.

Fund manager An organization that invests money on behalf of someone else.

Futures An agreement to buy or sell an asset at a certain time in the future for a certain price.

Gearing The characteristic of derivatives which enables a far greater reward for the same, or much smaller, initial outlay. It is the ratio of exposure to investment outlay, and is also known as leverage.

Gilt Domestic sterling-denominated long-term bond backed by the full faith and credit of the UK and issued by the Treasury.

Gilt-edged market-makers (GEMMs) A firm that is a market maker in gilts. Also known as a primary dealer.

Gilt-edged security UK government borrowing.

Give-up The process of giving a trade to a third party who will undertake the clearing and settlement of the trade.

Global clearing The channelling of the settlement of all futures and options trades through a single counterparty or through a number of counterparties geographically located.

Global custodian Institution that safekeeps, settles and performs processing of income collection, tax reclaim, multicurrency reporting, cash management, foreign exchange, corporate action and proxy monitoring etc. for clients' securities in all required marketplaces.

Global depository receipt (GDR) A security representing shares held in custody in the country of issue.

Good delivery Proper delivery of certificates that are negotiable and complete in terms of documentation or information.

Gross A position which is held with both the bought and sold trades kept open.

GSCC Government Securities Clearing Corporation – clearing organization for US Treasury securities.

Guaranteed bond Bonds on which the principal or income or both are guaranteed by another corporation or parent company in case of default by the issuing corporation.

Haircut The discount applied to the value of collateral used to cover margins.

Hedging A trading method which is designed to reduce or mitigate risk. Reducing the risk of a cash position in the futures instrument to offset the price movement of the cash asset. A broader definition of hedging includes using futures as a temporary substitute for the cash position.

Holder A person who has bought an open derivatives contract.

Immobilization The storage of securities certificates in a vault in order to eliminate physical movement of certificates/documents in transfer of ownership.

Independent clearing organization The independent organization is quite separate from the actual members of the exchange, and will guarantee to each member the performance of the contracts by having them registered in the organization's name.

Initial margin The deposit which the clearing house calls as protection against a default of a contract. It is returnable to the clearing member once the position is closed. The level is subject to changes in line with market conditions.

Institutional investor An institution which is usually investing money on behalf of others. Examples are mutual funds and pension funds.

Interest rate futures Based on a debt instrument such as a government bond or a Treasury bill as the underlying product and require the delivery of a bond or bill to fulfil the contract.

Interest rate swap An agreement to exchange interest related payments in the same currency from fixed rate into floating rate (or vice versa) or from one type of floating rate to another.

Interim dividend Dividend paid part-way through a year in advance of the final dividend.

International depository receipt (IDR) Receipt of shares of a foreign corporation held in the vaults of a depository bank. The receipt entitles the holder to all dividends and capital gains. Dividends and capital gains are converted to local currency as part of the service. IDRs allow investors to purchase foreign shares without having to involve themselves in foreign settlements and currency conversion.

International equity An equity of a company based outside the UK but traded internationally.

International petroleum exchange (IPE) Market for derivatives of petrol and oil products.

International securities identification number (ISIN) A coding system developed by the ISO for identifying securities. ISINs are designated to create one unique worldwide number for any security. It is a 12-digit alphanumeric code.

Interpolation The estimation of a price or rate, usually for a broken date, from two other rates or prices, each of which is for a date either side of the required date.

Intra-day margin An extra margin call which the clearing organization can call during the day when there is a very large movement up or down in the price of the contract.

Intrinsic value The amount by which an option is in-the-money.

Investment services directive (ISD) European Union Directive imposing common standards on investment business.

Investments Items defined in the FSA 1986 to be regulated by it. Includes shares, bonds, options, futures, life assurance and pensions.

Invoice amount The amount calculated under the formula specified by the futures exchange which will be paid in settlement of the delivery of the underlying asset.

IOSCO International Organization of Securities Commissions.

IPMA International Primary Markets Association.

Irredeemable gilt A gilt with no fixed date for redemption. Investors receive interest indefinitely.

ISDA International Swaps and Derivatives Association, previously known as the International Swap Dealers Association. Many market participants use ISDA documentation.

ISMA International Securities Markets Association.

ISSA The International Securities Services Association.

Issuer Legal entity that issues and distributed securities.

Issuing agent Agent (e.g. bank) who puts original issues out for sale.

JASDEC Japan Securities Depository Centre – the CSD for Japan.

JSCC Japan Securities Clearing Corporation – clearing organization in Japan.

Last notice day The final day that notification of delivery of a futures contract will be possible. On most exchanges all outstanding short futures contracts will be automatically delivered to open long positions.

Last trading day Often the day preceding last notice day which is the final opportunity for holders of long positions to trade out of their positions and avoid ultimate delivery.

LCH London Clearing House.

Leverage The magnification of gains and losses by only paying for part of the underlying value of the instrument or asset; the smaller the amount of funds invested, the greater the leverage. It is also known as gearing.

LIBID The London inter-bank bid rate. The rate at which one bank will lend to another.

LIBOR The London inter-bank offered rate. It is the rate used when one bank borrows from another bank. It is the benchmark used to price many capital market and derivative transactions.

LIFFE London International Financial Futures and Options Exchange.

Liquidity A liquid asset is one that can be converted easily and rapidly into cash without a substantial loss of value. In the money market, a security is said to be liquid if the spread between bid and asked price is narrow and reasonable size can be done at those quotes.

Liquidity risk The risk that a bank may not be able to close out a position because the market is illiquid.

Listed securities Securities listed on a stock exchange are tradeable on this exchange.

Loan stock *See* **Bonds**.

London Inter-Bank Offer Rate (LIBOR) Rate at which banks lend to each other which is often used as the benchmark for floating rate loans (FRNs).

London International Financial Futures and Options Exchange (LIFFE) Market for trading in bond, interest rate, FT-SE 100 index and FT-SE Mid 250 index, futures, plus equity options and soft commodity derivatives.

London Metal Exchange (LME) Market for trading in derivatives of metals such as copper, tin, zinc, etc.

London Stock Exchange (LSE) Market for trading in securities. Formerly know as the International Stock Exchange of the UK and Republic of Ireland or ISE.

Long A bought position in a derivative which is held open.

Long-dated Gilts with more than 15 years until redemption.

Long position Refers to an investor's account in which he has more shares of a specific security than he needs to meet his settlement obligations.

Lot The common term used to describe the standard unit of trading for futures and options. It is also referred to as a 'contract'.

Mandatory event A corporate action which affects the securities without giving any choice to the security holder.
Margin *Initial margin* is collateral placed by one party with a counterparty or clearing house at the time of a deal, against the possibility that the market price will move against the first party, thereby leaving the counterparty with a credit risk. *Variation margin* is a payment made, or collateral transferred, from one party to the other because the market price of the transaction or of collateral has changed. Variation margin payment is either in effect a settlement of profit/loss (for example, in the case of a futures contract) or the reduction of credit exposure. In a loan, margin is the extra interest above a benchmark such as LIBOR required by a lender to compensate for the credit risk of that particular borrower.
Mark-to-market The process of revaluing an OTC or exchange-traded product each day. It is the difference between the closing price on the previous day against the current closing price. For exchange traded products this is referred to as variation margin.
Market Description of any organization or facility through which items are traded. All exchanges are markets.
Market counterparty A person dealing as agent or principal with the broker and involved in the same nature of investment business as the broker. This also includes fellow members of the FSA or trading members of an investment exchange for those products only where they are members.
Market-maker A trader who works for an organization such as an investment bank. They quote bids and offers in the market and are normally under an obligation to make a price in a certain number of contracts. They create liquidity in the contract by offering to buy or sell.
Market price In the case of a security, the market price is usually considered as the last reported price at which the stock or bond has been sold.
Market risk Also position risk. The risk that the market value of a position falls.
Market value The price at which a security is trading and could presumably be purchased or sold.

Master agreement This agreement is for OTC transactions and is signed between the client and the broker. It covers the basic terms under which the client and broker wish to transact business. Each individual trade has a separate individual agreement with specific terms known as a confirm.

Matching (comparison) Another term for comparison (or checking); a matching system to compare trades and ensure that both sides of trade correspond.

Maturity The date on which the principal or nominal value of a bond becomes due and payable in full to the holder.

Medium dated Gilts due to be redeemed within the next seven to fifteen years.

Model risk The risk that the computer model used by a bank for valuation or risk assessment is incorrect or misinterpreted.

Modified following The convention that if a settlement date in the future falls on a non-business day, the settlement date will be moved to the next following business day, unless this moves it to the next month, in which case the settlement date is moved back to the last previous business day.

Money market The market for the purchase and sale of short-term financial instruments. Short term is usually defined as less than one year.

Money rate of return Annual return as a percentage of asset value.

MOF The Ministry of Finance (Japan).

Multilateral netting Trade between several counterparties in the same security are netted such that each counterparty makes only one transfer of cash or securities to another party or to a central clearing system. Handles only transactions due for settlement on the same day.

Mutual collateralization The deposit of collateral by both counterparties to a transaction.

NASDAQ National Association of Securities Dealers Automated Quotation system.

Netting Trading partners offset their positions thereby reducing the number of positions for settlement. Netting can be *bilateral*, *multilateral* or *continuous net settlement*.

Net asset value (NAV) In mutual funds, the market value of the fund share. It is common practice for an investment trust to compute its assets daily, or even twice a day, by totalling the closing market value of all securities and assets (i.e. cash) owned. All liabilities are deducted, and the balance is divided by the number of shares outstanding. The resulting figure is the net asset value per share.

Net present value (NPV) The net total of several present values (arising from cashflows at different future dates) added together, some of which may be positive and some negative.

Nil paid rights price Ex-rights price less the subscription price.

Nominal amount Value stated on the face of a security (principal value, par value). Securities processing: number of securities to deliver/receive.

Nominal value of a bond The value at which the capital, or principal, of a bond will be redeemed by the issuer. Also called par value.

Nominal value of a share The minimum price at which a share can be issued. Also called par value.

Nominee An organization that acts as the named owner of securities on behalf of a different beneficial owner who remains anonymous to the company.

Non-callable Cannot be redeemed by the issuer for a stated period of time from date of issue.

Non-clearing member A member of an exchange who does not undertake to settle their derivatives business. This type of member must appoint a clearing member to register all their trades at the clearing organization.

Non-cumulative preference share If the company fails to pay a preference dividend the entitlement to the dividend is simply lost. There is no accumulation.

Non-private customer A person who is not a private customer or who has requested to be treated as a non-private customer.

Nostro reconciliation Checking the entries shown on the bank's nostro account statement with the bank's internal records (the accounting ledgers) to ensure that they correspond exactly.

Note Bonds issued with a relatively short maturity are often called notes.

Notional Contracts for differences require a notional principal amount on which settlement can be calculated.

Novation The process where registered trades are cancelled with the clearing members and substituted by two new ones – one between the clearing house and the clearing member seller, the other between the clearing house and the clearing member buyer.

NSCC National Securities Clearing Corporation – clearing organization for US shares.

OASYS Trade confirmation system for US brokers operated by Thomson Financial Services.

Obligation netting An arrangement to transfer only the net amount (of cash or a security) due between two or more parties, rather than transfer all amounts between the parties on a gross basis.

Off-balance sheet A transaction whose principal amount is not shown on the balance sheet because it is a contingent liability or settled as a contract for differences.

Offer price The price at which a trader or market-maker is willing to sell a contract.

Offshore Relates to locations outside the controls of domestic monetary, exchange and legislative authorities. Offshore may not necessarily be outside the national boundaries of a country. In some countries, certain banks or other institutions may be granted offshore status and thus be exempt from all or specific controls or legislation.

Omnibus account Account containing the holdings of more than one client.

On-balance sheet A transaction whose principal amount is shown on the balance sheet.

On-line Processing which is executed via an interactive input onto a PC or stationary terminal connected to a processing centre.

Open outcry The style of trading whereby traders face each other in a designated area such as a pit and shout or call their respective bids and offers. Hand signals are also used to communicate. It is governed by exchange rules.

Open interest The number of contracts both bought and sold which remain open for delivery on an exchange. Important indicator for liquidity.

Open position The number of contracts which have not been off set at the clearing organization by the close of business.

Opening trade A bought or sold trade which is held open to create a position.

Operational risk The risk of losses resulting from inadequate systems and control, human errors or management failings.

Option An option is in the case of the *buyer*; the right, but not the obligation, to take (call) or make (put) for delivery of the underlying product and in the case of the *seller*; the obligation to make or take delivery of the underlying product.

Option premium The sum of money paid by the buyer for acquiring the right of the option. It is the sum of money received by the seller for incurring the obligation, having sold the rights, of the option. It is the sum of the intrinsic value and the time value.

Optional dividend Dividend that can be paid either in cash or in stock. The shareholders entitled to the dividend make the choice.

Options on futures These have the same characteristics as an option, the difference being that the underlying product is either a long or short futures contract. Premium is not exchanged, the contracts are marked to market each day.

Order-driven market A stock market where brokers acting on behalf of clients match trades with each other either on the trading floor of the exchange or through a central computer system.

Out-of-pocket expenses Market charges which are charged to the client without taking any profit.

Out-trade A trade which has been incorrectly matched on the floor of an exchange.

Over-the-counter (OTC) A one-to-one agreement between two counterparties where the specifications of the product are completely flexible and non-standardized.

Over-the-counter trading Trading made outside a stock exchange.

Pair off Back-to-back trade between two parties where settlement occurs only by exchanging the cash difference between the two parties.
Par value *See* **Nominal value**.
Pari passu Without partiality. Securities that rank *pari passu*, rank equally with each other.
Paying agent A bank which handles payment of interest and dividends on behalf of the issuer of a security.
Payment date Date on which a dividend or an interest payment is scheduled to be paid.
Perpetual bond A bond which has no redemption date.
Portfolio List of investments held by an individual or company, or list of loans made by a bank or financial institution.
Premium An option premium is the amount paid upfront by the purchaser of the option to the writer.
Present value The amount of money which needs to be invested (or borrowed) now at a given interest rate in order to achieve exactly a given cashflow in the future, assuming compound reinvestment (or refunding) of any interest payments received (or paid) before the end. *See* **Future value**.
Pre-settlement Checks and procedures undertaken immediately after execution of a trade prior to settlement.
Principal protected product An investment whose maturity value is guaranteed to be at least the principal amount invested initially.
Principal-to-principal market A market where the clearing house recognizes only the clearing member as one entity, and not the underlying clients of the clearing member.
Principal trading When a member firm of the London Stock Exchange buys stock from or sells stock to a non-member.
Principal value That amount inscribed on the face of a security and exclusive of interest or premium. It is the one used in the computation of interest due on such a security.
Private customer An individual person who is not acting in the course of carrying on investment business.
Proprietary trader A trader who deals for an organization such as an investment bank taking advantage of short-term price movements

as well as taking long-term views on whether the market will move up or down.

Put option An option that gives the buyer the right, but not the obligation, to sell a specified quantity of the underlying asset at a fixed price, on or before a specified date. The seller of a put option has the obligation (because they have sold the right) to take delivery of the underlying asset if the option is exercised by the buyer.

Quote driven Dealing system where some firms accept the responsibility to quote buying and selling prices.

Range forward A forward outright with two forward rates, where settlement takes place at the higher forward rate if the spot rate at maturity is higher than that, at the lower forward rate if the spot rate at maturity is lower than that, or at the spot rate at maturity otherwise.

RCH Recognized clearing house under FSMA 2000.

Real-time gross settlement (RTGS) Gross settlement system where trades are settled continuously through the processing day.

Realized profit Profit which has arisen from a real sale.

Recognized investment exchange (RIE) Status required by FSMA 2000 for exchanges in the UK.

Reconciliation The comparison of a person's records of cash and securities position with records held by another party and the investigation and resolution of any discrepancies between the two sets of records.

Record date The date on which a securities holder must hold the securities in order to receive an income or entitlement.

Redemption The purchase and cancellation of outstanding securities through a cash payment to the holder.

Redemption price A price at which bonds may be redeemed, or called, at the issuer's option, prior to maturity (often with a slight premium).

Registered bond A bond whose owner is registered with the issuer or its registrar.

Registered title Form of ownership of securities where the owner's name appears on a register maintained by the company.

Registrar An official of a company who maintains its share register.

Registrar of companies Government department responsible for keeping records of all companies.

Replacement cost The mark-to-market loss which would be incurred if it were necessary to undertake a new transaction to replace an existing one, because the existing counterparty defaulted.

Repurchase agreement (repo) Borrowing funds by providing a government security for collateral and promising to 'repurchase' the security at the end of the agreed upon time period. The associated interest rate is the 'repo-rate'.

Reputational risk The risk that an organization's reputation will be damaged.

RIE Recognized investment exchange under FSA 1986.

Rights issue Offer of shares made to existing shareholders.

Right of offset Where positions and cash held by the clearing organization in different accounts for a member are allowed to be netted.

Risk warning Document that must be despatched and signed by private customers before they deal in traded options.

Roll-over A LIBOR fixing on a new tranche of loan, or transfer of a futures position to the next delivery month.

Rolling settlement System used in most countries including England. Bargains are settled a set number of days after being transacted.

Safekeeping Holding of securities on behalf of clients. They are free to sell at any time.

SCL Settlement organization and custodian of Spanish securities.

Scrip dividends Scrip dividends options provide shareholders with the choice of receiving dividend entitlements in the form of cash, share or a combination or both. The amount of stocks to be distributed under a scrip option is calculated by dividing the cash dividend amount by the average market price over a recent period of time.

Scrip issue *See* **Bonus issue**.

SEATS Plus An order-driven system used on the London Stock Exchange for securities which do not attract at least two firms of market-makers and for all AIM securities.

Secondary market Marketplace for trading in existing securities. The price at which they are trading has no direct effect on the company's fortunes but is a reflection of investors' perceptions of the company.

Securities Bonds and equities.

Securities house General term covering any type of organization involved in securities although usually reserved for the larger firms.

Securities lending Loan of securities by an investor to another (usually a broker-dealer), usually to cover a short sale.

Securities and futures authority (SFA) Prior to the FSA assuming its full powers, it was the SRO responsible for regulating securities and futures firms.

Securities and investments board (SIB) Former name of the Financial Services Authority.

SEDOL Stock Exchange Daily Official List, a securities numbering system assigned by the International Stock Exchange in London.

Segregated account Account in which there is only the holdings of one client.

Segregation of funds Where the client assets are held separately from those assets belonging to the member firm.

Self-regulating organizations (SROs) Bodies which receive their status from FSA and are able to regulate sectors of the financial services industry. Membership of an SRO provides authorization.

SEQUAL The checking system used for international equities.

SETS London Stock Exchange Trading System.

Settlement The fulfilment of the contractual commitments of transacted business.

Settlement date The date on which a trade is cleared by delivery of securities against funds (actual settlement date, contractual settlement date).

Share option A right sold to an investor conferring the option to buy or sell shares of a particular company at a predetermined price and within a specified time limit.

Short A sold position in a derivative which is held open.

Short coupons Bonds or notes with a short current maturity.

Short cover The purchase of a security that has been previously sold short. The purpose is to return securities that were borrowed to make a delivery.

Short-dated gilt Gilts due to be redeemed within the next seven years, according to the LSE (FT states up to 5 years).

Short sale The sale of securities not owned by the seller in the expectation that the price of these securities will fall or as part of an arbitrage.

Short selling Selling stock that you do not own.

Short-term security Generally an obligation maturing in less than one year.

SICOVAM CSD for French corporate securities and OATs (now merged with Euroclear).

Simple interest Interest calculated on the assumption that there is no opportunity to re-invest the interest payments during the life of an investment and thereby earn extra income.

SIS SEGA Inter Settle – CSD for Switzerland.

Soft commodities Description given to commodities such as sugar, coffee and cocoa, traded through LIFFE since its incorporation of the former London Commodity Exchange (LCE).

Sovereign debt securities Bonds issued by the government of a country.

SPAN Standardized Portfolio Analysis of Risk. A form of margin calculation which is used by various clearing organizations.

Speculation A deal undertaken because the dealer expects prices to move in his favour and thereby realize a profit.

Speculator The speculator is a trader who wants to assume risk for potentially much higher rewards.

Sponsored member Type of CREST member whose name appears on the register but has no computer link with CREST.

Spot delivery A delivery or settlement of currencies on the value date, two business days later.

Spot market Market for immediate as opposed to future delivery. In the spot market for foreign exchange, settlement is in two business days ahead.

Spot month The first month for which futures contracts are available.

Spot rate The price prevailing in the spot market.

Spread (1) The difference between bid and asked price on a security. (2) Difference between yield on or prices of two securities of different types or maturities. (3) In underwriting, difference between price realized by an issuer and price paid by the investor. (4) Difference between two prices or two rates. What commodities traders would refer to as the basis.

Stamp duty Tax on purchase of equities in the UK.

Stamp Duty Reserve Tax (SDRT) (UK) Tax payable on the purchase of UK equities in uncertified form (i.e. those held within CREST).

Standard settlement instructions Instructions for settlement with a particular counterparty which are always followed for a particular kind of deal and, once in place, are therefore not repeated at the time of each transaction.

Standing instruction Default instruction, e.g. provided to an agent processing payments or clearing securities trades; provided by shareholder on how to vote shares (for example, vote for all management recommended candidates).

Stanza di compensazione Italian clearing organization.

Stock In some countries (e.g. the USA), the term applies to ordinary share capital of a company. In other countries (e.g. the UK), stock may mean share capital that is issued in variable amount instead of in fixed specified amounts, or it can describe government loans.

Stock dividend Dividends paid by a company in stock instead of cash.

Stock Exchange Automated Quotation System (SEAQ) Electronic screen display system through which market-makers in equities display prices at which they are willing to deal.

Stock Index Futures/Options Based on the value of an underlying stock index such as the FTSE 100 in the UK, the S&P 500 index in the USA and the Nikkei 225 and 300 in Japan. Delivery is fulfilled by the payment or receipt of cash against the exchange calculated delivery settlement price. These are referred to as both indices or indexes.

Stock (order) An owner of a physical security that has been mutilated, lost or stolen will request the issuer to place a stop (transfer) on the security and to cancel and replace the security.

Stock (or bond) power A legal document, either on the back of registered stocks and bonds or attached to them, by which the owner assigns his interest in the corporation to a third party, allowing that party the right to substitute another name on the company records instead of the original owner's.

Stock split When a corporation splits its stock, it divides.

Straight debt A standard bond issue, without right to convert into the common shares of the issuer.

Straightthrough processing Computer transmission of the details of a trade, without manual intervention, from their original input by the trader to all other relevant areas – position keeping, risk control, accounts, settlement, reconciliation.

Street name Securities held in street name are held in the name of a broker or another nominee, i.e. a customer.

Strike price The fixed price, per share or unit, at which an option conveys the right to call (purchase) or put (sell) the underlying shares or units.

Strike price/rate Also exercise price. The price or rate at which the holder of an option can insist on the underlying transaction being fulfilled.

Stripped bonds (strips) Bonds where the rights to the interest payments and eventual repayment of the nominal value have been separated from each other and trade independently. Facility introduced for gilts in December 1997.

Sub-custodian A bank in a foreign country that acts on behalf of the custodian as its custody agent.

Subscription price Price at which shareholders of a corporation are entitled to purchase common shares in a rights offering or at which subscription warrants are exercisable.

Subscriptions In a bond issue, the buying orders from the lead manager, co-managers, underwriters and selling group members for the securities being offered.

Stump period A calculation period, usually at the beginning or end of a swap, other than the standard ones normally quoted.

Swap Arrangement where two borrowers, one of whom has fixed interest and one of whom has floating rate borrowings, swap their commitments with each other. A bank would arrange the swap and charge a fee.

SwapClear A clearing house and central counterparty for swaps.

SwapsWire An electronic dealing system for swaps.

SWIFT Society for Worldwide Interbank Financial Telecommunications – secure electronic communications network between banks.

TARGET Trans European Automated Real time Gross settlement Express Transfer – system linking the real-time gross settlements for euros in the 15 European Union countries.

Tax reclaim The process that a global custodian and/or a holder of securities performs, in accordance with local government filing requirements, in order to recapture an allowable percentage of tax withheld.

Termination date The end date of a swap.

Thomson Report An electronic transaction reporting system for international equities on the London Stock Exchange operated by Thomson.

Tick size The value of a one-point movement in the contract price.

Time value The amount by which an option's premium exceeds its intrinsic value. Where an option has no intrinsic value the premium consists entirely of time value.

Trade date The date on which a trade is made.

Trade guarantees Guarantees in place in a market which ensure that all compared or netted trades will be settled as compared regardless of a counterparty default.

Traded option An option which is traded on an exchange.

Trader An individual who buys and sells securities with the objective of making short-term gains.

Transfer agent Agent appointed by a corporation to maintain records of stock and bond owners, to cancel and issue certificates and to resolve problems arising from lost, destroyed or stolen certificates.

Transfer form Document which owners of registered documents must sign when they sell the security. Not required where a book entry transfer system is in use.

Transparency The degree to which a market is characterized by prompt availability of accurate price and volume information which gives participants comfort that the market is fair.

TRAX Trade confirmation system for the Euromarkets operated by ISMA.

Treasury bill Money market instrument issued with a life of less than one year issued by the US and UK governments.

Treasury bonds (USA) US government bond issued with a 30-year maturity.

Treasury notes (USA) US government bond issued with 2-, 3-, 5- and 7-year maturity.

Triple A rating The highest credit rating for a bond or company – the risk of default (or non-payment) is negligible.

Trustee A person appointed to oversee the management of certain funds. They are responsible for ensuring that the fund is managed correctly and that the interests of the investor are protected and that all relevant regulations and legislation are complied with.

Turnaround Securities bought and sold for settlement on the same day.

Turnaround time The time available or needed to settle a turnaround trade.

Underlying asset The asset from which the future or option's price is derived.

Undersubscribed Circumstance when people have applied for fewer shares than are available in a new issue.

Unrealized profit Profit which has not arisen from a sale – an increase in value of an asset.

Value at Risk (VaR) The maximum amount which a bank expects to lose, with a given confidence level, over a given time period.

Variation margin The process of revaluing an exchange-traded product each day. It is the difference between the closing price on the previous day against the current closing price. It is physically paid or received each day by the clearing organization. It is often referred to as the mark-to-market.

Volatility The degree of scatter of the underlying price when compared to the mean average rate.

Warrant An option which can be listed on an exchange, with a lifetime of generally more than one year.

Warrant agent A bank appointed by the issuer as an intermediary between the issuing company and the (physical) warrant holders, interacting when the latter want to exercise the warrants.

Withholding tax In the securities industry, a tax imposed by a government's tax authorities on dividends and interest paid.

Writer A person who has sold an open derivatives contract and is obliged to deliver or take delivery upon notification of exercise from the buyer.

XETRA Dealing system of the Deutsche Börse.

Yield Internal rate of return expressed as a percentage.

Yield curve For securities that expose the investor to the same credit risk, a graph showing the relationship at a given point in the time between yield and current maturity. Yield curves are typically drawn using yields on governments of various maturities.

Yield to maturity The rate of return yielded by a debt security held to maturity when both interest payments and the investor's capital gain or loss on the security are taken into account.

Zero coupon bond A bond issued with no coupon but a price substantially below par so that only capital is accrued over the life of the loan, and yield is comparable to coupon-bearing instruments.

Index

SECURITIES INSTITUTE

Qualifications

Securities Institute Diploma – the professional qualification for practitioners leading to Fellowship of the Institute

Investment Advice Certificate – the benchmark examination for financial advisors

SFA Registered Persons Examination – the benchmark examinations for employees of SFA regulated firms

Investment Administration Qualification – the benchmark examination for administration, operations and IT staff

International Capital Markets Qualification – the introductory qualification for overseas and emerging markets

Membership

Professionalism through a progressive structure of recognized designations: SIAff, MSI, FSI

Over 17,000 students, affiliates, members and fellows

Free membership events, providing education and networking opportunities

Examination qualification programmes

Continuing Learning opportunities through a wide range of courses and conferences with discounts available for members

Training, Continuing Learning & Publications for the financial services industry

The courses, seminars and publications we produce are researched and developed by working closely with market practitioners and employers to produce focussed, high quality and value-for-money training solutions that meet the needs of busy professionals.

To find out more about all our products and services, please call the Marketing Department on *020 7645 0670*, email us on *marketing@securities-institute.org.uk*, or visit our web site:

www.securities–institute.org.uk

Centurion House, 24 Monument Street, London, EC3R 8AQ

PROFESSIONALISM | INTEGRITY | EXCELLENCE

Printed in the United States
206146BV00003B/10/P

9 780750 654869